The Conquest of Constantinople

ROBERT OF CLARI

Translated with introduction and notes
by Edgar Holmes McNeal

COLUMBIA UNIVERSITY PRESS
NEW YORK

Columbia University Press
Publishers Since 1893
New York   Chichester, West Sussex
Copyright © 1936, 2005 Columbia University Press
All rights reserved

Library of Congress Cataloging-in-Publication Data
Clari, Robert de, 12th / 13th cent.
   [Conquête de Constantinople. English]
   The Conquest of Constantinople / Robert of
Clari ; translated with introduction and notes by
Edgar Holmes McNeal.
        p.   cm. — (Records of Western civilization)
   Includes bibliographical references (p.) and index.
   Translated from Old French.
   ISBN 0–231–13668–4 (cloth : alk. paper) —
     0–231–13669–2 (pbk. : alk. paper)
   1. Istanbul (Turkey) — History — Siege,
1203–1204. 2. Crusades — Fourth, 1202–1204.
I. McNeal, Edgar Holmes, 1874– . II. Title.
III. Series.

D164.A3C54513 2005
945.5'03 — dc22
                              2004061381

∞

Columbia University Press books are printed on
permanent and durable acid-free paper.
Printed in the United States of America
c 10 9 8 7 6 5 4 3 2 1
p 10 9 8 7 6 5 4 3 2

RECORDS OF WESTERN CIVILIZATION

The Art of Courtly Love, by Andreas Capellanus. Translated with an introduction and notes by John Jay Parry.

The Correspondence of Pope Gregory VII: Selected Letters from the Registrum. Translated with an introduction by Ephraim Emerton.

Medieval Handbooks of Penance: The Principal Libri Poenitentiales and Selections from Related Documents. Translated by John T. McNeill and Helena M. Gamer.

Macrobius: Commentary on The Dream of Scipio. Translated with an introduction by William Harris Stahl.

Medieval Trade in the Mediterranean World: Illustrative Documents. Translated with introductions and notes by Robert S. Lopez and Irving W. Raymond, with a foreword and bibliography by Olivia Remie Constable.

The Cosmographia *of Bernardus Silvestris*. Translated with an introduction by Winthrop Wetherbee.

Heresies of the High Middle Ages. Translated and annotated by Walker L. Wakefield and Austin P. Evans.

The Didascalicon *of Hugh of Saint Victor: A Medieval Guide to the Arts*. Translated with an introduction by Jerome Taylor.

Martianus Capella and the Seven Liberal Arts.

    Vol. I: *The Quadrivium of Martianus Capella: Latin Traditions in the Mathematical Sciences*, by William Harris Stahl with Richard Johnson and E. L. Burge.

    Vol. II: *The Marriage of Philology and Mercury*, by Martianus Capella. Translated by William Harris Stahl and Richard Johnson with E. L. Burge.

The See of Peter, by James T. Shotwell and Louise Ropes Loomis.

Two Renaissance Book Hunters: The Letters of Poggius Bracciolini to Nicolaus de Niccolis. Translated and annotated by Phyllis Walter Goodhart Gordan.

Guillaume d'Orange: Four Twelfth-Century Epics. Translated with an introduction by Joan M. Ferrante.

Visions of the End: Apocalyptic Traditions in the Middle Ages, by Bernard McGinn, with a new preface and expanded bibliography.

The Letters of Saint Boniface. Translated by Ephraim Emerton, with a new introduction and bibliography by Thomas F. X. Noble.

Imperial Lives and Letters of the Eleventh Century. Translated by Theodor E. Mommsen and Karl F. Morrison, with a historical introduction and new suggested readings by Karl F. Morrison.

An Arab-Syrian Gentleman and Warrior in the Period of the Crusades: Memoirs of Usāmah ibn-Munqidh. Translated by Philip K. Hitti, with a new foreword by Richard W. Bulliet.

De expugnatione Lyxbonensi (The Conquest of Lisbon). Edited and translated by Charles Wendell David, with a new foreword and bibliography by Jonathan Phillips.

Defensor pacis. Translated with an introduction by Alan Gewirth, with an afterword and updated bibliography by Cary J. Nederman.

History of the Archbishops of Hamburg-Bremen. Translated with an introduction and notes by Francis J. Tschan, with a new introduction and bibliography by Timothy Reuter.

The Two Cities: A Chronicle of Universal History to the Year 1146, by Otto, Bishop of Freising. Translated in full with an introduction and notes by Charles Christopher Mierow, with a foreword and updated bibliography by Karl F. Morrison.

The Chronicle of Henry of Livonia, by Henricus Lettus. Translated and with a new introduction and notes by James A. Brundage.

Lanzelet, by Ulrich von Zatzikhoven. Translated with a new introduction by Thomas Kerth, with additional notes by Kenneth G. T. Webster and Roger Sherman Loomis.

The Deeds of Frederick Barbarossa, by Otto of Freising. Translated and annotated with an introduction by Charles Christopher Mierow with the collaboration of Richard Emery.

Giles of Rome's On Ecclesiastical Power: *A Medieval Theory of World Government*. A Critical edition and translation by R. W. Dyson.

The Conquest of Constantinople. Robert of Clari. Translated with introduction and notes by Edgar Holmes McNeal.

The Murder of Charles the Good. Galbert of Bruges. Translated and edited by James Bruce Ross.

Foreword

THE chronicle of Robert of Clari has not received the attention it deserves, mainly because it has been overshadowed by the well-known work of his compatriot, Geoffrey of Villehardouin. The first satisfactory printed edition of the text appeared in 1924, and there is no translation in a modern language, except for a few extracts in French and German. The present translation is offered in the confident hope that readers will find it interesting not only as an independent eyewitness account of the Fourth Crusade, but even more as a rare human document. For the author was an ordinary knight who underwent strange experiences and saw many marvels, and had them recorded in his own naïve and simple words.

In making the translation, the writer has used a photograph of the manuscript and the manuscript itself at Copenhagen, as well as the printed editions of the text, and especially the excellent edition of M. Philippe Lauer, to whom he makes grateful acknowledgment. He wishes also to express his gratitude for the kindness and helpfulness of Miss Ellen Jörgensen and Mr. J. Bonnesen and the staff of the Royal Library of Copenhagen, and of M. Pierre Dubois and the staff of the Municipal Library of Amiens. He is indebted above all to the editor of the series, Professor Austin P. Evans of Columbia University, for constant help and guidance in the preparation of the work.

EDGAR HOLMES MCNEAL

COLUMBUS, OHIO
January, 1936

Contents

The Conquest of Constantinople

Introduction

Introduction

MONG the many remarkable episodes of the crusading age, perhaps the most astounding was the exploit of those French knights and Venetian seamen who set out to rescue the Holy Land and ended by capturing Constantinople. This expedition, known to modern historians as the Fourth Crusade, is memorable also for the number of contemporary accounts which it inspired.[1] One of these is the story dictated by Robert of Clari, a simple, obscure knight of Picardy, who was a member of the crusading host and shared its experiences.

Robert of Clari names himself as the author in the concluding paragraph or envoy of his chronicle: "Now you have heard the truth, how Constantinople was conquered . . . as he bears witness who was there and saw it and heard it, Robert of Clari, knight." He also mentions himself once in the course of the narrative, by name and in the third person, in relating an incident that redounded to the glory of his brother, Aleaumes

---

[1] The best known and most valuable is the chronicle of Geoffrey of Villehardouin, written in old French from the dictation of one who was intimately involved in all the events of the expedition. The *Devastatio Constantinopolitana* is a brief anonymous account, accurate and circumstantial, the work apparently of a follower of the marquis Boniface (but see Kandel in *Byzantion*, IV, 179-88). The *Historia Constantinopolitana* was composed by Gunther, a monk in the Cistercian monastery of Pairis in Alsace, for the purpose of authenticating the relics which Abbot Martin brought back from Constantinople. The same motive inspired the brief *Peregrinatio in Graeciam*, incorporated in the annals of Halberstadt and apparently based on the account of Bishop Conrad. Aside from these chronicles dealing with the expedition by itself, there are a number of contemporary accounts in works of a larger scope, such as Nicetas' voluminous history of the Byzantine emperors, the Old French history of the kingdom of Jerusalem (cited as the *Continuation of William of Tyre* or as *Ernoul*, and incorporated in the great composite history of the crusades known as the *Livre d'Eracles*), the *Gesta Innocentii tertii*, a biography of the pope, and the general Latin chronicles of Robert of Auxerre, Alberic of Trois-Fontaines, Ralph of Coggeshall, and others.

the priest. His chronicle implies very clearly that he was a vassal of Pierre of Amiens, and this fact is established beyond doubt by other contemporary evidence. Thus he was one of the knights who served under Pierre's banner. He fought in the division that was under the joint command of Pierre and his cousin Hugh, count of St. Pol, in the battle outside the land walls of Constantinople in July, 1203; he was one of the small band led by Pierre in the attack on the postern gate at the time of the great assault of April, 1204; and he was apparently in the expedition led by Emperor Baldwin to Salonika, on the return from which Pierre died.

Robert seems to have come back to his native land early in 1205. The chronicle really ends with the disaster of Adrianople, April, 1205, in which Emperor Baldwin was defeated and taken prisoner. The subsequent events to 1216 are told in an epilogue that covers less than two pages of the manuscript, and even the account of the preparations for the expedition to Adrianople does not read like that of an eyewitness. It has been conjectured that after the death of Pierre of Amiens in the summer of 1204, his followers were united with the contingent of Hugh of St. Pol, and that after the latter's death in March, 1205, they returned home.[2]

The identity of Robert of Clari has been definitely established in recent times by the discovery of deeds in which his name occurs.[3] The family name was taken from Clari, now Cléry-lez-Pernois, in the commune of Pernois. This with other small holdings made up the little fief which Robert, like his father Gilo before him, held as a vassal of Pierre of Amiens. This Pierre was descended from the castellans of Amiens and

[2] The time of Robert's return is involved in the question of the date of composition of the chronicle. Fullest discussion of this is found in Wanner, *Robert de Clari, ein altfranzösischer Chronist des IV. Kreuzzuges*, pp. 77 ff., who concludes that Robert left Constantinople between March 9 and March 29, 1205. A good summary of the arguments is given by Lauer, *Robert de Clari, La Conquête de Constantinople*, pp. vii f.

[3] Boudon, "Robert de Clari en Aminois," *Bulletin de la Société des antiquaires de Picardie*, XIX (1895-97), 700-734; and "Documents nouveaux sur la famille de Robert de Clari," *ibid.*, XX (1899), 372-79.

was connected with the powerful family of the counts of St. Pol. Gilo of Clari and his son Robert, knights (*milites*), appear as witnesses in a deed of gift issued by Pierre of Amiens in 1202 and in another deed of the same year issued by the bishop of Amiens.

That one Robert of Clari went to Constantinople on this expedition and returned home, is attested also by certain relics which once existed in the church of St. Pierre of the monastery of Corbie. In a work published in 1665, Du Cange described a reliquary in the form of a cross, on which there was an inscription in Old French giving a list of the relics contained in it and stating that they came from the Holy Chapel of the imperial palace of Constantinople and had been brought by "Robillard of Clari in that time when Baldwin, count of Flanders, was emperor."[4] Dom Coquelin, in his history of the abbey of Corbie,[5] describes the same reliquary as a silver cross in the center of which was a piece of the True Cross. A description of the religious treasures of Corbie, written about the same time, mentions another reliquary in the form of a crystal cross, which contained a piece of the True Cross together with particles of the Crown of Thorns, the Sudarium, and the Sponge, and which had on the base a Latin inscription: *Bene sit Robillardo qui me attulit Constantinopoli.*[6] Both crosses were described again and in greater detail at the end of the eighteenth century by Dom Grenier in his history of Corbie.[7]

[4] *Traité historique du chef de S. Jean-Baptiste.* The text of the inscription is reproduced from Du Cange in Riant, *Exuviae*, II, 175-76; see also Lauer, p. vi.

[5] *Historiae regalis abbatiae Corbeiensis compendium.* Dom Benedict Coquelin was *officialis*, or presiding judge of the monastery court, from 1672 to 1678.

[6] *Histoire abrégée du trésor de l'abbaye royale de St. Pierre de Corbie.* According to the modern editor, H. Dusevel, this is a copy of an inventory preserved in the Bibliothèque Nationale.

[7] *Histoire de la ville et du comté de Corbie*, printed in 1910 for the Société des antiquaires de Picardie. Of the first he says: "This cross, twenty-two inches in height, is of silver with gold filigree; in the center there is a cross four inches in height by three inches across, made of the wood of the True Cross. . . . The other relics are placed in the extremities of the

Except for the pieces of the True Cross, the relics themselves must have been very small objects, since they were placed in the small cavities at the extremities of the reliquary crosses. They were evidently such shreds or fragments, taken from the sacred objects, as were usually made into packets or "bourses" for returning pilgrims. It is not surprising to find that one of the knights who took part in the capture of Constantinople was able to bring back a little sacred booty of this sort. There is, however, a piece of written evidence which seems to indicate something very different. The Bibliothèque Municipale of Amiens possesses a long rolled parchment, which contains an inventory of the treasure of Corbie in two parts. The second part is a later addition to the original list, drawn up in 1283. It is entitled: *Sanctuarium quod Robertus de Clari, miles, attulit Constantinopoli.* This describes a veritable treasure chest, including a large number of gold, silver, and crystal reliquaries, and such important relics as "half of the girdle of the Blessed Virgin, the arm of St. Mark the Evangelist, the finger of St. Helena." It is impossible to conceive of Robert of Clari, a simple knight, bringing back a treasure of this extent. The explanation is undoubtedly to be found in the error of the maker of the inventory, who carelessly or ignorantly attributed, in his title, all the contents of the chasse to the person whose name he found inscribed on two of the reliquaries in it.[8]

The last event mentioned by Robert is the death of Emperor Henry, June, 1216. As already noted, however, the events

cross." Of the other he says: ". . . another cross of rock crystal . . . in which is inclosed the wood of the True Cross. One can read on the extremities of the crystal cross, which are covered with plaques of silver and enamel, *de sudario Domini, de cruce Domini, de spongia Domini,* and on the base: *Beins ait Robillar qui m'apporta de Costentinople.*" Dom Grenier evidently misread the inscription, supposing it to be Old French.

[8] This inventory was first cited by Dom Coquelin in his *Compendium* (pp. 506 ff.) and is reproduced by Riant in his *Exuviae* (II, 197-99). Both of these accepted the evidence of the title at its face value. Riant (*Dépouilles,* III° partie, sec. 14) drew from it the conclusion that Robert of Clari was a special envoy of Emperor Baldwin, commissioned to convey a great treasure of relics to the monastery of Corbie—as indeed he must have been if he really brought back all the treasures listed in the document!

from 1205 to 1216 are summed up very briefly in what appears to be an epilogue to the main story. This may be explained in either of two ways: (1) that Robert dictated his account as one piece shortly after 1216, treating the events subsequent to his own return from Constantinople in a summary fashion; or (2) that he dictated it soon after his return home and then added the epilogue in 1216, after hearing of the death of Emperor Henry.[9] On the whole, the former hypothesis is the simpler and more natural one, especially as there are no time references in the body of the chronicle requiring any part of it to have been written before 1216.[10]

The Manuscript and Its Transmission

It is almost by accident that we possess the chronicle of Robert of Clari. The original writing, made by a scribe at Robert's dictation, has completely disappeared. It was apparently deposited in the once famous Benedictine monastery of Corbie, the great religious institution of the region. About 1300 some scribe in the monastery was entrusted with the task of copying into a single volume certain Old French manuscripts belonging to the library. This was due probably to the fact that the separate manuscripts were deteriorating through use or neglect and were in danger of becoming illegible. The result was a beautiful vellum book of 128 leaves, with two narrow columns to a page. Four of the works thus preserved were of a known value and vogue at the time. These were: the popular chronicle

[9] This is the view adopted by Wanner in the work mentioned above, note 2. His arguments, however, are not very convincing (see note 128 to the translation).

[10] Nothing is known of Robert's life after 1216. Riant (*Exuviae*, I, clxxxviii) makes the unwarranted assumption that he became a monk in the monastery of Corbie. This was apparently the point of departure for the free fancy of Bouchet (*Geoffroi de Villehardouin*, II, 302): "As for Robert, he returned in 1213, old before his time, discouraged and disillusioned, bringing back to the abbey of Corbie, where he took the frock, the precious relics which were the only reward he was ever to obtain"! Boudon ("Documents nouveaux") found the family of Clari mentioned among the documents of the bishopric of Amiens as late as 1390.

to which the modern editor De Wailly has given the title
Récits d'un ménestrel de Reims; a translation by John of
Flixecourt of the Latin poem known as Dares the Phrygian's
De excidio Troiae; a translation of the *Chronicle of Turpin;*
a translation of the well-known Latin treatise the *Disciplina
clericalis* of Petrus Alphonsus.[11]

The fifth part of the book is Robert's chronicle. It begins
on folio 100 verso, folio 100 recto being blank, and ends on
folio 128 recto. Thus it covers 56 pages of two columns each.
Interesting as it is to the modern student of history, it did not
have the claims to preservation as a work important for a
monastery library to possess, which were shared by the other
four. Its inclusion in the book seems, therefore, to have been
more or less fortuitous, and may have been due, as was so often
the case in medieval bookmaking, to the desire of the scribe
to use up the quires of precious vellum assigned to him. This
impression is strengthened by the character of the writing,
which is evidently the work of a different and inferior though
quite contemporaneous hand. The letters are much less care-
fully formed and the copyist has crowded 38 lines into his
columns, while all other parts have 37 lines to a column. One
is tempted to conjecture that the scribe to whom the task was
assigned entrusted this part to a subordinate, as being less important than the others.

The vellum book containing a copy of Robert's chronicle
seems to have remained in the library of Corbie until the end

---

[11] This text of the *Disciplina clericalis* has been published by Hilka and
Söderhjelm (*Petri Alfonsi disciplina clericalis,* II. *Französischer Prosatext,*
1912). De Wailly seems not to have known the text of the *Récits* contained
in our manuscript; its relation to the texts which he used in his edition is
discussed by Nyrop in *Romania,* VIII (1879), 429-33. The chronicle of
Turpin was originally translated by Renaut, count of Boulogne, in 1206 and
was later copied by Michael Harnes, who changed the wording of the
prologue so as to credit himself with the translation; the text in our manuscript belongs to this later group; see Gaston Paris, *De pseudo-Turpino,* 1865.
As to the date of the manuscript: John of Flixecourt says he made his translation in 1262; Nyrop says that this text of the *Récits* is later than 1286;
and the editors of the *Disciplina* place the translation at about the turn of the
century.

of the sixteenth century. About the middle of that century
Corbie had come under commendatory abbots who were care-
less of its treasures and allowed the library to be despoiled of
many of its manuscripts. Dom Coquelin refers in his history
of Corbie to the "pious thefts" of distinguished scholars of his
time, mentioning such names as Masson, Sirmond, and Du
Chesne. It was probably in this manner that our manuscript
began its wanderings. We know that it came into the hands
of the French scholar and amateur of manuscripts Paul Pétau
(died 1614), who made a note and wrote his name on the last
page,[12] and of the Danish scholar Petrus Scavenius, who sold
it with the rest of his library to the king of Denmark in 1664.[13]
Since that time, it has remained in the safekeeping of the Royal
Library at Copenhagen.

[12] On leaf 128 recto, in the margin of the last column, one reads: "Froissart parle d'un Sire de Clary, Volum. 2, ch. 136"; and at the end of the
column: "Pa. Pétau, Con^{er} en Parl." This note was due to a misunderstand-
ing on Pétau's part; there was, in fact, no connection between Froissart's
Sire de Clary and our Robert of Clari. Perhaps it was this note that led
Chambon ("Un Historien peu connu de la quatrième croisade," 1897) to
make the entirely erroneous statement that both Froissart and Villehardouin
mention Robert of Clari.

[13] See Bruun, Det store kongelige Bibliotheks Stiftelse, 1873. Two other
links in the chain are added by Quignon (Un Historien picard de la quatrième
croisade, 1908). He mentions Claude Fauchet as having possessed the
manuscript before Paul Pétau, and adds the name of the latter's son Alexandre
before that of Scavenius. It is said that the name of Claude Fauchet was
once visible at the top of the first page of the manuscript, written across the
words: Liber Sancti Petri Corbeiensis, but all that can be seen there now
is a badly blurred erasure under which no writing is decipherable. It is
quite probable that the manuscript was in the possession of Alexandre Pétau
between his father's death in 1614 and the purchase by Scavenius about 1650.
On the left-hand page of the third leaf of paper preceding the manuscript
in its present binding there is written, in a hand and a spelling of the sixteenth or seventeenth century, the following:

Traicté en vieux Gaulois de l'histoire de France
Les adventures de la Ruine de Troye
Des chastimens et des proverbes des philosophes
La prise de Constantinople.

This list of contents, from which the chronicle of Turpin has been omitted
by mistake, may have been written by one of the French owners of the
manuscript.

The first published description of the book appeared in 1786 in the catalogue of the manuscripts of the Royal Library at Copenhagen made by John Erichsen, librarian from 1778 to 1787.[14] Then in 1836 Georg Waitz visited Copenhagen on a tour of northern libraries and published a notice of our manuscript in an article in the *Archiv* for 1839.[15] This, however, was almost a verbal reproduction of Erichsen's notice. Finally, in 1844 N. C. L. Abrahams published a much fuller and more accurate description of the book.[16]

Editions of the Chronicle

These notices, especially that of Abrahams, called the attention of scholars to the existence of an independent and hitherto unused source for the Fourth Crusade, and it was to be expected that some one would soon undertake its publication. In 1855, Karl Hopf, a young German scholar then at the University of Bonn, secured the loan of the manuscript and made a copy of Robert's chronicle. It was his intention to include it in a collection of chronicles and documents of the Latin Empire of the East, a field in which he had already published some original studies. The project languished, however, and it was not until nearly twenty years later that his edition appeared in print in his *Chroniques gréco-romanes* (Berlin, 1873).[17]

[14] *Udsigt over den gamle Manuscript-Samling i det store kongelige Bibliothek*, Copenhagen, 1786.

[15] "Untersuchung der handschriftlichen Sammlungen zu Copenhagen im Herbste 1836," *Archiv der Gesellschaft für ältere deutsche Geschichtskunde*, VII (1839), 153.

[16] *Description des manuscrits français du moyen âge de la Bibliothèque Royale de Copenhague*, pp. 106 ff. He attempted to identify the works and gave the opening and closing lines of each.

[17] The circumstances are related by Hopf in his introduction, pp. vii ff.; see also the article of Rambaud, reprinted in the *Mémoires de l'Académie de Caen*, 1873, and the review of this article by Paul Meyer in the *Revue critique* (1872, 2d sem., 395-96). Hopf originally submitted his proposal to the French government, which agreed to undertake it, but as he failed to furnish the texts the matter was dropped. Much later he decided to publish his collection in Germany.

In the meantime, the French scholar Count Paul Riant had become interested in the chronicle of Robert of Clari, and despairing, as Hopf not ungenerously says, of ever seeing in print the latter's long announced edition, determined to publish the chronicle himself. In 1868 the text was finished and in type, and a few copies were struck off, of which one was deposited with the Bibliothèque Nationale[18] and others were presented to friends of the author. This contained only the text, without title page, introduction, or notes. Apparently Riant later became dissatisfied with the text, which was in fact very faulty, and decided to destroy the copies still in the hands of the printer, although a few copies, as has been noted, were already in circulation. In this abortive enterprise the chronicle of Robert of Clari first saw the light in printed form.[19]

In 1873 the first real edition of the chronicle appeared in Hopf's *Chroniques gréco-romanes* (pp. 1-85). The text was not free from errors,[20] but it was usable and was supplied with an historical introduction and with a few notes giving for the most part rather obvious historical identifications. This edition, while not entirely satisfactory, nevertheless held the field for more than fifty years.

Finally, in 1924, an excellent edition appeared in the series "Les Classiques français du moyen âge." This was made by M. Philippe Lauer, librarian of manuscripts in the Bibliothèque Nationale. The series in which it appeared, however, is primarily for the use of students of French language and literature, and the texts are provided with only the necessary minimum of historical apparatus. The present writer, there-

[18] Notice in the *Bibliothèque de l'École des chartes*, XXX (1869), 723, and XXXII (1872), 315-16.

[19] The notice of Riant's text in the *Bibliothèque de l'École des chartes* (1872) is too favorable by half; it speaks of it as a "complete and correct edition, in spite of the provisional character to which the modesty of the author has condemned it." On the other hand, Nyrop (*Zeitschrift für romanische Philologie*, III, 1879, 96-98) is too severe in saying that "it swarms with errors and is worthless for anyone who would use the chronicle for purposes of research."

[20] Paul Meyer added a page of corrections at the end of the volume, and Nyrop pointed out others in the article referred to in the preceding note.

fore, has felt justified in attempting to supply, in introduction and notes, a somewhat fuller setting for the chronicle of Robert of Clari.

Value of the Chronicle as an Historical Source

We meet at the outset two questions arising from the relation of the manuscript to Robert's dictation: (1) did the copyist make a correct copy of the manuscript in front of him? and (2) did the first scribe content himself with putting Robert's account into writing without changing it? It is not possible, of course, to give a categorical answer to either question. As to the first, there are a few lapses, such as repetitions, omissions, misreadings, and blanks, but not enough to convict the copyist of gross carelessness.[21] As to the second, we can only say that the content, vocabulary, and style are all quite compatible with a verbal transcription of Robert's words—there is nothing in it that might not well be the dictation of a simple unlettered knight such as he appears to have been.[22]

Assuming that we have substantially the account dictated by Robert of Clari, we must next consider its importance as a history of the expedition. Obviously, not all parts are of equal value. The first section, down to the gathering of the crusaders at Venice in the summer of 1202, seems to have been based largely on stories heard later in camp and on the route.[23] On

[21] These will be noted where they affect the translation. Lauer has indicated some of them in his "Notes critiques" (pp. 110-11). Jeanroy (*Romania*, LIII, 392 ff.) points out others and suggests emendations.

[22] Quignon (*Un Historien picard*) held that Robert's account was revised by the monks of Corbie, in order to enhance the value of the relics which the monastery possessed, but there is no evidence in the chronicle itself of such interposition.

[23] This is shown very clearly by a comparison of his account with that of Villehardouin, whose authority in this part is not to be questioned. Robert places the embassy to Venice after the election of Marquis Boniface as leader of the host, which throws the whole story out of perspective. His account of the embassy reads like a popular tale. Klimke (*Quellen*, p. 9) makes the suggestion that Robert might have learned about the embassy from his compatriot, Alard Maquereau, who was one of the envoys, but this is very

the other hand, Robert's own knowledge of events in the East ended with his departure for home, probably just before the battle of Adrianople in April, 1205.

Between these limits (except for certain historical digressions which will be noted later), Robert was narrating events in which he himself had a part. His position, however, was that of the ordinary knight, and the critical events, the momentous decisions, took place on a plane above him, in the assemblies of counts and barons and in the inner councils of leaders.

The most important of these "high matters" was the decision of the leaders to go to Constantinople. Robert's treatment of this episode will illustrate his method of handling such events. If we may accept the official version presented by Villehardouin's chronicle and by the letters of the leaders,[24] the affair arose through the chance encounter of the disinherited Greek prince Alexius with bands of crusaders on their way to the rendezvous at Venice. The guardians of the youth, thinking they might secure the services of these forces in his cause, sent envoys to Venice to sound out the leaders of the crusade. The negotiations thus begun bore fruit later at Zara in an embassy sent by Alexius and his brother-in-law, the German emperor Philip of Swabia. In return for their aid in recovering his rights in Constantinople, Alexius promised to give the crusaders 200,000 marks, to send an army of 10,000 men with them in their attack on the Saracens, to maintain a permanent force of 500 knights in the Holy Land, and to bring the Greek Church into obedience to the pope. The leaders were moved to accept these offers, because the funds of the host were exhausted and they saw no other means of carrying out the crusade. They were

unlikely, since Robert apparently did not know that Alard was a member of the delegation, which he says was composed of Conon of Béthune and the marshal of Champagne.

[24] These letters were sent to the West right after the first occupation of Constantinople, when the prospects of the crusaders were at their brightest. One was a circular letter written in the name of all the leaders and the other was a letter of Hugh, count of St. Pol, to his friend Henry, duke of Louvain. These will be found in the Recueil des historiens des Gaules et de la France, XVIII, 515 ff.

led to believe also that the diversion of the expedition would
be only temporary, since they were assured by young Alexius
that all the Greeks were eager to welcome him back. So, in the
face of general opposition to the project, the leaders signed the
treaty, thus involving the expedition in unforeseen troubles at
Constantinople.[25]

Robert's account runs as follows: After spending the winter
at Zara, the crusaders found that they had reached the end of
their resources and despaired of being able to go on with the
crusade. Seeing their straits, the doge approached the leaders
and suggested that they could easily replenish their funds and
provisions in the neighboring rich land of Greece, if only they
had some good excuse for going there. Thereupon the marquis
arose and said that he had met last Christmas, at the court of
his lord the emperor, the young Greek prince Alexius. If they
could secure this youth they would have their good excuse for
going to Constantinople, since he was the rightful heir. So
they sent envoys to Germany for him, and young Alexius came
and joined the host at Corfu, whither the fleet had in the

---

[25] This explanation, presented by the persons who were responsible for
the decision, has something of the character of an apologetic. The statement
of facts is probably accurate, as far as it goes, but this does not exclude the
possibility of secret understandings and interested motives on the part of some
of the protagonists, such as the doge of Venice, the German emperor, and
the marquis. The "diversion question" was once the subject of a lively con-
troversy among scholars. Mas Latrie, in his history of Cyprus (1861), stated
that the Venetians had a secret understanding with the sultan of Egypt,
whereby they were to divert the crusade from his land in return for special
commercial privileges. This, however, was based on a very doubtful story
found in the Old French history of the kingdom of Jerusalem. Then Hopf,
in his *Geschichte Griechenlands* (1867), announced the discovery of the
treaty which proved the guilt of the Venetians. With this the chase was on,
and one scholar after another combed the records for evidence as to the
real villain of the piece. The foundations of these ingenious hypotheses were
weakened when Hanotaux in the *Revue historique* (1877) demonstrated that
Hopf's supposed discovery was nothing more than the commercial treaties between Venice and Egypt, which had not been negotiated until several years
after the crusade. The best summary of the dispute will be found in the
article by Gerland in the *Neue Jahrbücher* for 1904. See also Luchaire,
Innocent III; la question d'Orient (1907). The latest contribution is the
article of Vriens in *Tijdschrift voor Geschiednis*, 1922.

meantime proceeded. There he made them his offer (in much the same terms as those given in the other sources). The proposal was then submitted to the assembly of barons and a violent dispute arose. The marquis was more eager than anyone else that they should go to Constantinople, because he wanted to avenge the injury which the Greek emperor had done to his brother Conrad. Finally all the barons agreed to the proposal, and the fleet set sail for Constantinople.

As an explanation of the diversion, this account is evidently naïve and inadequate. Moreover, it contains some obvious inconsistencies. On the other hand, there are certain points on which Robert seems to have been quite well informed. The arguments for and against the proposal which he puts in the mouths of the speakers agree very closely with those given by Villehardouin and by Hugh of St. Pol, and his statement of the terms offered by Alexius are surprisingly accurate.

The materials from which Robert constructed his account are fairly obvious. The external events took place before his own eyes. Like the other members of the host, he was aware of the coming and going of envoys, of the arrival of important personages, of the bustle incident to the summoning of assemblies and councils of war. The camp was undoubtedly astir with rumors about the meaning of these events, and Robert's story about the marquis was probably only one of many tales which circulated among the knights and common people of the host. This body of half-information and conjecture was apparently supplemented by official proclamations, in which the leaders conveyed to the host the reasons for the change in direction.[26] Robert wove these various materials into his account, undertaking, like a good story-teller, to initiate his hearers into all the secrets of the action, without being unduly critical of his own sources of information.

About matters that came within the range of his own knowledge, Robert contributes many interesting details, which fill in the picture of the Fourth Crusade. Among these may be noted:

[26] The letter of Hugh of St. Pol refers to such a proclamation in the phrase *toti exercitui manifeste ostendantes.*

the flying bridges of the Venetian ships, the maneuvers of battalions in the skirmish before the land walls on July 17, 1203,
the religious preparation and incitement to battle on the Sunday
before the great assault, the attack on the postern gate on April
12, 1204, and the magnificent scene at the coronation of Emperor Baldwin. Especially noteworthy is his condemnation of
the "high men" (the counts and barons) for robbing the knights
and common people of the host of a fair share in the spoils
of Constantinople. He refers more than once to their greed
and injustice, and draws from the disaster at Adrianople this
moral: "Thus did God take vengeance on them for their pride
and for the bad faith which they kept with the poor people of
the host, and for the terrible sins which they committed in the
city after they had taken it."

In some ways the most interesting part of Robert's chronicle
is his description of the marvels of Constantinople. In any
event, it is unique. No other French or Latin chronicler among
those who visited Constantinople, in this time or earlier, bethought himself to describe the city in such detail—not Liut-
prand of Cremona, nor Odo of Deuil, nor William of Tyre,
nor Villehardouin. It may be said that all these visitors had
other things to think about while they were in the city, but
we may be glad that Robert had the leisure to take in, open-
eyed and open-mouthed, the wonders he saw and heard in Constantinople.

He was, of course, the innocent sight-seer and not the trained
archaeologist; nevertheless his account is remarkable for its
general accuracy. The buildings and monuments are plainly
recognizable—the Great Palace, Saint Sophia, the Hippodrome,
the equestrian statue of Justinian, the Golden Gate, and the
"pictured" columns. So, too, he is correct in his locating of
famous relics—the True Cross and other relics of the Passion
in the church of the Blessed Virgin in the Great Palace, the
Column of Flagellation and the bodies of apostles and of Constantine and Helena in the church of the Holy Apostles, the
slab on which the body of Our Lord was laid, in the abbey of
the Pantocrator.

Robert embellishes his description of the marvels of Constantinople with stories that he heard about them, apparently from Greek guides and interpreters. These have to do either with the precious relics and their miraculous properties or with the buildings and monuments. Among the former are some interesting examples of religious legends. The loin cloth of the holy man which received the imprint of Our Lord's features is a variant of the famous legend of the "Image of Edessa." The painting of St. Demetrius which constantly exuded a healing oil is an example of a familiar type of wonder-working relic. The *sydoine* which miraculously opened out every Friday to display the portrait of Our Lord, appears to be a confusion between the *sindon*, or grave cloth, and the *sudarium*, or napkin, the True Image of St. Veronica.

The tales Robert heard about the monuments of the city are such as would naturally grow up among the native Greek inhabitants. They are the products of mistaken identifications reflecting local pride as well as ignorance, imaginary interpretations of inscriptions that could not be read by the unlettered, and traditions of a glorious and romantic past.

It is noteworthy that the medieval populace of Constantinople, like the medieval populace of Rome, was ignorant of its antique past and gave wrong names to monuments—for example, the equestrian statue of Justinian, which was pointed out to Robert as the statue of the emperor Eracles (Heraclius, conqueror of Chosroes and recoverer of the True Cross). The story of the Golden Gate, which was opened only for the triumphal entry of an emperor returning from a victorious campaign, reflects an ancient and true tradition. Popular pride must have given rise to the supposed inscriptions, as the one on the equestrian statue ("letters which said that he swore the Saracens never should have truce from him"), and that on the statue above the Gate of the Golden Mantle ("anyone who lives in Constantinople a year can have a mantle of gold just as I have"), and those on the two bronze female statues, which Robert's informant must have taken sardonic delight in interpreting for him. What more characteristic piece of popular archaeology can be found than the explanation of the two "pictured" columns: that the bands of figures and letters were really prophecies of future events, only the prophecies were never understood until after the event—and even this last disaster, the capture of the city by the French, was prefigured and foretold there. Characteristic, too, is the marvelous tale of the statues of men and beasts in the Hippodrome that used to go through motions by enchantment, but did not do so any more. Tall tales told by the Greeks of Constantinople to the simple-minded traveler from the West!

In the course of his narrative of the expedition, Robert indulges in two digressions of considerable length, one dealing with former Byzantine emperors and the other with the exploits of Conrad of Montferrat. These purport to explain, respectively, the origins of Isaac and young Alexius, and the reason why the marquis hated the Greek emperor. In fact, they are introduced for their own sake, as entertaining tales that would embellish the chronicle.

The Byzantine interlude begins with an anecdote about the emperor Manuel. It tells of the predilection of this emperor for "those of the law of Rome," and especially for the French, and of the discontent which this aroused among the Greeks of his court. To silence the grumblers, the emperor, with the connivance of the French, staged a skirmish between the two groups, in which the Greeks ran away. Thereupon the emperor called in the Greek lords and forbade them ever again to complain of his largesse and his fondness for the French, whom he proposed henceforth to favor more than ever. There is this element of truth in the tale, that Manuel was known to be a liberal patron of French nobles and soldiers of fortune, and prided himself on possessing the qualities of western chivalry. Aside from this, the tale is a parable of the cowardice of the Greeks and the valor of the French, based perhaps on some real incident.[27] One can easily imagine the rise and growth of

[27] Pauphilet ("Sur Robert de Clari," *Romania*, LVII, 295) suggests that the "false departure" of the French is a distorted reflection of the expulsion of the Venetians in 1171 by Manuel and their subsequent return. This is

a good story of this sort among the French population of Constantinople, and the telling of it to the crusaders encamped there.

After a brief account of the events leading to the usurpation of Emperor Andronicus, we come to the principal part of this interlude, the story of Andronicus and Isaac Angelus. This, too, has all the marks of a popular tale, arising in this case among the Greeks of Constantinople, and based upon a real incident. In 1185 the unspeakable Andronicus was overthrown by an insurrection and Isaac Angelus was raised to the imperial throne. Andronicus fled but was recaptured and brought back to Constantinople, where he was publicly subjected to torture until he died. These tragic and terrible events gave rise to a romantic story, from which the Greek historian Nicetas seems to have borrowed the legendary features found in his account.[28] A version half-way between that of Nicetas and that of Robert is found in the Old French history of Jerusalem.[29] The story appears also in the English chronicle of Benedict of Peterborough,[30] in a wildly distorted form. Robert seems to have heard the tale in Constantinople, and probably from the French residents of the city.

The other historical interlude is the saga of Conrad of Montferrat. It consists of two parts: Conrad in Constantinople, and Conrad in the Holy Land, both of which are based on historical facts. The first part tells of Conrad setting out on the Third Crusade with two galleys and stopping off at Constantinople. Just then the city was being besieged by a rebellious lord, "li Vernas" (Alexius Branas), and the emperor besought Conrad to help him. Raising a force from his own followers and from the Latins of Constantinople, Conrad sallied forth to attack

---

most unlikely, since the tale is told not of Italian traders and merchants but of French nobles in the court and army. Chalandon (*Jean II Comnène*, p. 226) cites William of Tyre and Nicetas for Manuel's fondness for the French.

[28] Nicetas, pp. 440 ff. See the writer's article, "The Story of Isaac and Andronicus," in *Speculum*, IX (1934), 324-29.

[29] *Recueil des historiens des croisades; historiens occidentaux*, II, 18 ff.

[30] Edited by Stubbs, Rolls Series, XLIX, i, 255 ff.

the enemy, and the emperor treacherously closed the gates behind him. Conrad attacked the besieging army, putting it to flight and slaying Branas with his own hand, and then returned to the city to reproach the emperor for his treachery. Warned that the latter was conspiring to have him slain, he escaped from the city with his two galleys and sailed to the Holy Land.

The Old French history of Jerusalem has an account of the visit of Conrad to Constantinople which resembles that of Robert except that it does not imply any treachery on the part of the emperor. In the fuller and presumably older version,[31] the name of the emperor is given as Alexius (Alexius III, 1195-1203). This is an error, since Conrad really visited Constantinople in 1187, when Isaac was emperor. The compiler of the abbreviated form, represented by Mas Latrie's *Chronique d'Ernoul*, corrected this by transposing the incident to its proper place immediately after the coronation of Isaac. Robert evidently heard the older version, since he supposes the emperor of the tale to have been Alexius III, the one ruling in 1203, when the marquis urged the expedition to Constantinople.

A detailed and circumstantial account of the revolt of Branas and the visit of Conrad of Montferrat is given by Nicetas. The point to the tale as he tells it is the inertia and pusillanimity of Isaac. As is well known, Nicetas, in this part of his history, written after the fall of Constantinople, is inspired with patriotic scorn and contempt for the Angeli and their hangers-on, who were responsible in his eyes for the fate that befell the "Empress of Cities."

The rest of this interlude deals with the exploits of Conrad in the Holy Land. If we compare it with the best source for these events, the Old French history of the kingdom of Jerusalem, we see that Robert again is telling a popular tale, or historical romance, with Conrad of Montferrat as its hero. This would develop most naturally among the followers and com-

---

[31] The "Estoire de Eracles empereur," published in the *Recueil des historiens des croisades*. The complicated problem of the manuscripts of this work has not been seriously reconsidered since Mas Latrie's "Essai de classification," first published in 1860 and reprinted in his edition of the Chronicle of Ernoul in 1871.

patriots of Conrad, some of whom Robert would encounter in the host or in camp at Constantinople.[32]

Robert's Qualities as a Chronicler

In the preceding section we considered Robert's opportunities for knowing the events which he narrated. We must now try to make an estimate of his qualities as a chronicler, his veracity, his prejudices and prepossessions.[33]

In the first place, it should be said to his credit that Robert had no axe of his own to grind. He was not concerned, like Villehardouin, with justifying the actions of the responsible leaders; nor, like Gunther, with authenticating precious relics brought back from Constantinople; nor, like the author of the Old French history of the Holy Land, with exposing the unworthy motives of the crusaders and the imaginary treason to Christendom of the Venetians. Moreover, he did not dictate his chronicle in order to preserve to posterity a record of his own exploits. He does not tell us about the fine motives that led him to take the cross, nor expatiate on his own brave deeds. As already noted, he mentions himself just once in the narrative, and then in a very subordinate rôle. He does, to be sure, refer more than once to his brother Aleaumes the priest, listing him among those who did most deeds of prowess and of arms, describing his heroism at the breach in the walls, and telling how he boldly asserted the rights of the priests to be reckoned as equal to the knights in the division of spoils. But his fraternal pride and affection is merely an incidental (and engaging) note in the general tone of his chronicle.

Robert's general credibility as a witness, in those matters which he records from his own knowledge, is established by a

---

[32] It is significant that Robert's romantic story of the coronation of Guy of Lusignan turns up again a generation later in that collection of romanticized historical anecdotes, the *Récits d'un ménestrel de Reims*.

[33] See the brief but admirable summary by Lauer, Introduction, pp. viii ff.; see also the articles by Pauphilet, "Robert de Clari et Villehardouin," in *Mélanges-Jeanroy*, pp. 559 ff., and "Sur Robert de Clari," in *Romania*, LVII, 289-311.

comparison with other sources, wherever the comparison is possible. His accounts of the capture of the harbor and of the great assault by the fleet on the sea walls agree in detail with the chronicle of Villehardouin. The maneuvers of the forces in front of the land walls, when the emperor declined the battle, are told by Robert from his own position in one of the attacking divisions, but his account can be fitted perfectly into the more general descriptions given by Villehardouin and by Hugh of St. Pol. There is one incident, reported by Villehardouin, which Robert must have known about but of which he makes no mention. Villehardouin lists Robert's own lord, Pierre of Amiens, among the disgruntled barons who prepared to leave the host at Corfu. If Robert followed his lord in this move, perhaps he preferred not to remember it later.

Robert naturally shared the prejudices and prepossessions which were common to his time and race and station. He had a low opinion of the Greeks, as cowardly and treacherous by nature, an opinion which a century of unhappy contacts between crusading Europe and Constantinople had made a commonplace in the West. Apparently he was not greatly disturbed by the fact that they were schismatics; it was not Robert but the bishops and other preachers who denounced them as enemies of God and worse than Jews because they were disobedient to the law of Rome. He does not betray any strong feeling, one way or the other, toward the Venetians. He seems to see the doge as a staunch bourgeois, for whom the expedition was primarily an enterprise for profit—willing to drive a hard bargain and to bluster and threaten his unfortunate debtors, but willing also to compromise and make the best of a bad bargain. He gives him credit for wisdom and foresight in the conduct of affairs. He seems to have had a respect for the doge's sturdiness of character; at least, he relates with considerable gusto the doge's words and actions in scolding the leaders for their incompetence in the matter of the payment for the fleet, in refusing to be overawed by the threat of papal excommunication in the affair of Zara, and in berating the faithless Alexius. In fact, the doge's is the most complete and consistent portrait that emerges from Robert's chronicle.

It is possible, perhaps, to detect a certain prejudice against the marquis Boniface. In Robert's account of the diversion to Constantinople, he shows the marquis as willing to engage the host in the enterprise in order to satisfy a personal grudge against the Greek emperor. It was the marquis who was mainly responsible for the trouble over the election of an emperor, by his determination to pack the electoral commission with his own men, and it was the marquis who was the more to blame in the quarrel with Emperor Baldwin over Salonika. In all this Robert was presumably reflecting the opinion of his companions, the French knights of the host, and there may have been in it something of the prejudice of the French toward a non-French prince.

Such prejudices as Robert may have had come out in an impersonal way, in the narrative of events, and not in his own recriminations. In fact, there was just one matter in which he allowed his personal feelings to appear—the unfair treatment of the knights and common people by the high men of the host in the division of spoils. This still rankled in his breast when he dictated his story of the Fourth Crusade.

The Chronicle in Old French Literature and Historiography

The *genre* to which Robert's chronicle belongs is indicated not inaptly in his own words in prologue and envoy: "Here begins the history of those who conquered Constantinople"; "Now you have heard the truth how Constantinople was conquered . . . and if he has not told (*contee*) the conquest as finely as many a good teller (*diteeur*) would have told it, nevertheless he has told the very truth." This is an *estoire*, a *conte*, a true history recounted in the simple manner of the prose tale. The work deserves to be considered in relation to the development of prose narration in Old French, and to the growth of interest in history on the part of feudal society.

As is well known, the appearance of Old French prose is a phenomenon of the thirteenth century. The twelfth century had seen the growth and flowering of narrative poetry, from the epics of rude feudal warfare like the *Chanson de Roland* to the romances of chivalry and courtesy of Chrétien de Troyes. Narrative prose had not yet appeared in writing, but we can scarcely doubt that it already existed in oral form. Poets and minstrels must often have introduced their recitals with prose summaries of preceding events, and may very likely have included in their repertories prose romances like that of *Aucassin et Nicolette*, which was put in writing in the early thirteenth century.

The interest of feudal society in history is evidenced by the epic poetry of the twelfth century itself. These poems were histories in a way, since they purported to recount real events of the past and the deeds of historical personages. Thus they appealed to the historical sense as well as to the warlike or courtly tastes of their hearers. They dealt, of course, with a remote and legendary past, with the age of Charlemagne, of Alexander, or of King Arthur. In the later twelfth century we encounter narrative poems treating of past events more nearly concerning the feudal audience, like the epic of the Norman Conquest, the *Roman de Rou* of the Norman poet Wace. At the very end of the century we find a real chronicle in verse of recent events in the poem recounting the crusade of Richard Lionheart, the *Estoire de la guerre sainte* of the Anglo-Norman minstrel Ambroise.

The Old French chronicle has its literary roots in these two earlier forms: the prose tale told to entertain an audience and the narrative poem dealing with actual historical events. The new type appeared in three works that were virtually contemporaneous, the chronicle of Villehardouin, the Old French history of the kingdom of Jerusalem, and the chronicle of Robert of Clari.[34] All of them employ the simple narrative style and

[34] Villehardouin's chronicle ends in 1207 and Robert's in 1216. The date of composition of the Old French history of Jerusalem is uncertain,

devices of the prose tale or *conte*. The narrator begins at the beginning, in the simple manner of the fairy tale: "Once upon a time there was a king." He addresses his hearers directly, calling their attention to important incidents about to be told and warning them of impending transitions in the action: "Now you shall hear of a great deed of prowess"; "Now give ear to a great marvel"; "I forgot to tell you about a certain matter"; "Now we shall leave off telling about this affair and tell you about this other." He dramatizes the incidents of the story, presenting them as dialogues in the words of the participants, as if he had been present at the scenes.

Of the three, Robert's chronicle is the simplest and most naïve in its style and diction. Thus his narrative method is the closest to that of the oral tale. It seems as if he must have heard tales beginning with a prologue and ending with an envoy and employing devices to hold the attention of hearers. It may have been at home in his own circle, where he heard minstrels recite tales of "the time of Alexander or the time of Charlemagne" (to which he refers in his estimate of the wealth of Constantinople), or of Troy the Great, which once belonged to the ancestors of the French, as he makes Pierre of Bracheux boast to Joannissa. He certainly heard the recent history of the Byzantine emperors and of Conrad of Montferrat recounted in this manner by story-tellers in the camp at Constantinople. Wherever he got it, it was the model of the *conte* that he had in his mind when he set out to dictate his chronicle.

In respect to vocabulary, Robert's prose is inferior to that of either of the other two chroniclers with whom he must be compared. Nevertheless, his equipment is not inadequate to his task as chronicler of the crusade. He is familiar with the current terminology of the crusades; Fulk of Neuilly "preaches the cross"; the crusaders are the "crossed" (*croisie*) or "pilgrims"; the objective is the "Holy Land of oversea." As is to be expected, he is familiar with the technical terms of feudal warfare—military maneuvers, arms and armor, wall defenses,

---

but an abbreviated form (Mas Latrie's *Ernoul*) was already known in the West by 1231.

and siege engines. He also has a fair vocabulary of naval terms, which he may have acquired on the expedition. He knows the correct terms for the various ranks of feudal society and for the ordinary customs and usages. He has the familiarity with ecclesiastical terms that might be expected of a layman of his station. It was perhaps at Constantinople that he learned to speak of patriarch and icon (which he reproduces as *ansconne*), of camels and elephants, of jasper, porphyry, and gold mosaic (*ore musike*). He refers to Greek officials by their French equivalents (*bailli, serjans, uissiers*), and uses for Greek proper names and place names the forms current in the West: Kyrsac for Isaac, Morchofles for Alexius Ducas Murzuphlus, Bras St. Jorge for the Straits, and Babyloine for Cairo.

The Translation

It has been the purpose of the translator to give as far as possible a literal translation of the text. He has departed from this practice only rarely, when literalness would result in confusion of meaning or in too great awkwardness. Occasionally the meaningless repetition of words in the same sentence has been suppressed; so when the text has: "This palace was so rich and noble that no one could describe to you the great nobility and richness of this palace," it has seemed permissible to translate the last words: "its great nobility and richness." A similar liberty has been taken in cases where the narrative shifts from past to historical present and back again, in the same sentence. Even such harmless interventions have been resorted to only sparingly. In general, the translator has resisted the temptation to use more complex or more varied constructions or to find synonyms for words too frequently used; for the simple style and meager vocabulary seemed to belong of right to the author —to be qualities of which he should not be despoiled. Certain favorite locutions (*si grant que trop, fist molt grant feste, si ne fait mais el*, etc.,) have been rendered in each case by what seemed to be the nearest idiomatic phrase in English, the words of the text and the literal meaning being given in a footnote where the locution first occurs.

Feudal titles are given their English forms: knight, count, marquis, marshal, advocate. Like other Old French chroniclers of the age, Robert uses the French form *dux* (acc. *duc*) for the ruler of Venice, but it has seemed better to render this by the Italian "doge," as less confusing than "duke." Given names are generally rendered by English equivalents, Baldwin, Hugh, Henry, John, William; on the other hand, the French forms Pierre and Thibaut have somehow seemed more in keeping with the tone of the chronicle than Peter and Theobald. Names of Greek emperors and other historical persons are given the usual English forms: Manuel, Isaac, Alexius, Murzuphlus, Lascaris, Branas. The same practice has been followed in geographical names, Jadres, Bouke d'Ave, la Filee, Coine, being rendered Zara, Abydos, Philea, Konia. In all these cases the form given in the text is indicated in a footnote.

Text

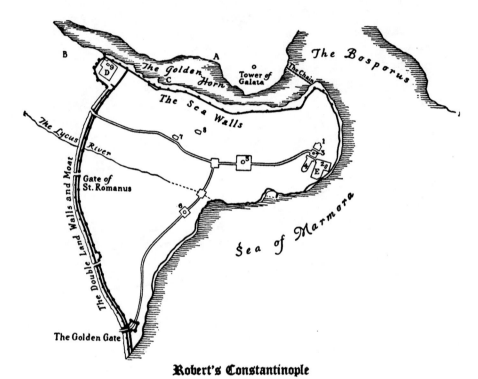

Robert's Constantinople

A. Quarters of the Crusaders and Venetians across the Golden Horn
B. Terrain of the Battle of July 17, 1203
C. Place of the Great Attack on the Sea Walls, April 12, 1204
D. The Palace of Blachernae
E. The Great Palace (Boukoleon, Bouke de Lion)

1. Saint Sophia. 2. The Church of the Virgin of the Pharos (the Holy Chapel). 3. Column and Equestrian Statue of Justinian (Eracles the Emperor). 4. The Hippodrome (the Games of the Emperor). 5. Column of Theodosius. 6. Column of Arcadius. 7. The Church of the Holy Apostles. 8. The Church of Christ Pantocrator. 9. The Church of the Virgin of Blachernae.

¶ **Here begins the prologue of Constantinople, how it was taken; afterwards you shall hear why they went there.**[1]

ERE begins the history of those who conquered Constantinople, and afterwards we shall tell you who they were and for what reason they went there. It happened, in that time when Pope Innocent was apostolic[2] of Rome and Philip was king of France and there was another Philip who was emperor of Germany and the year of the incarnation was one thousand two hundred and three or four,[3] that there was a priest, Master Fulk[4] was his name, who was of Neuilly, a parish which is in the bishopric of Paris. This priest was a right worthy man and a right good clerk, and he went through the land preaching the cross, and many people followed him because he was so worthy a man that God wrought great miracles for him. And this priest won much wealth to be carried to the Holy Land oversea. In that time Count Thibaut of Champagne was given the cross, and Baldwin, count of Flanders, and Henry his brother, and Louis, count of Blois, and Hugh, count of St. Pol, and Simon, count of Montfort, and Guy his brother. Next we shall name you the

---

[1] Each of the five works included in the manuscript has an introductory sentence written in red ink. These were apparently invented by the copyist to serve as titles and were not part of the manuscripts he was copying. In this case he has merely paraphrased the opening sentence of Robert's chronicle.

[2] *apostoiles*, the current synonym for pope in Old French (from the Latin *apostolicus*); so used in Villehardouin, in the Old French history of the kingdom of Jerusalem, and in the Old French translation of William of Tyre.

[3] Robert apparently had no notion of calendar years—it was in the summer of 1202 that he himself set out for Venice. Fulk had been preaching repentance for some years before receiving the papal authorization to preach the cross, at the hands of Cardinal Peter Capuano in November, 1198.

[4] *Foukes*. For Fulk of Neuilly, see Gutsch, "A Twelfth Century Preacher —Fulk of Neuilly," in *Crusades and Other Essays*, with references to the sources. Villehardouin, Gunther of Pairis, and the *Devastatio* also mention his preaching as the beginning of the crusade.

bishops who were there. There was the bishop Nivelon of Soissons, who was a very worthy man and valiant in every duty and in every need, and the bishop Warnier of Troyes and the bishop of Halberstadt[5] in Germany, and Master John of Noyon, who was elected to be the bishop of Acre. There was also the abbot of Loos in Flanders, which was one of the houses of the order of Cîteaux—this abbot was a right wise and a right worthy man—and other abbots and clerks so many that we cannot name you them all. And the barons who were there, we cannot name them all, but a part of them we can name you. From Aminois there was my lord Pierre of Amiens, the fair knight and the worthy and the valiant, and my lord Enguerrand of Boves, one of four brothers (one of them was named Robert, another Hugh, and the other brother was a clerk), Baldwin of Beauvoir, Matthew of Warlincourt, the advocate of Béthune, and Conon his brother,[6] Eustace of Canteleux, Anseau of Cayeux, Renier of Trit, Wales of Frise, Girard of Manchecourt, Nicholas of Mailly, Baldwin Cavarom, Hugh of Beauvais, and many other knights, high men, who were Flemings and of other countries, all of whom we cannot name you. And there was also my lord James of Avesnes. From Burgundy there was Odo of Champlitte and William his brother, who had many people in the host. And there were many others from Burgundy, all of whom we cannot name you. From Champagne there was the marshal[7] and Ogier of Saint-Chéron and Macaire of St.-Menehould and Clarembaux of Chappes and Miles of Brabant. These were from Champagne. Then there was the castellan of Coucy, and Robert of Ronsoi, Matthew of Montmorency, who was a right worthy man, Raoul of Aulnoy and

[5] *Hanetaist*, in the manuscript. This was Bishop Conrad.

[6] The French title *avoué* meant originally the patron or protector of a monastery. In the early feudal age this "protection" was often forced on the abbot by a powerful local lord as a means of getting possession of the monastery lands. Early in the eleventh century an ancestor of William and Conon of Béthune became the advocate of the rich monastery of St. Vaast in Arras. Conon of Béthune, mentioned here, was a poet of some reputation (see Wallensköld, *Les Chansons de Conon de Béthune*, 1921).

[7] Geoffrey of Villehardouin, the famous chronicler of the expedition.

Walter his son, Giles of Aulnoy, Pierre of Bracheux, the worthy knight and the hardy and the valiant, and Hugh his brother. Those whom I name you here were from France [8] and from Beauvaisis. From Chartrain there was Gervais of the Châtel and Hervé his son and Oliver of Rochefort and Pierre of Alost and Payen of Orleans, Pierre of Amiens,[9] a good knight and worthy and one who did many deeds of prowess there, and Thomas, a clerk, his brother, who was a canon of Amiens, Manasses of Lille in Flanders, Matthew of Montmorency, and the castellan of Corbie. Now there were so many other knights of France and of Flanders and of Champagne and of Burgundy and of other countries that we cannot name you them all, valiant knights and worthy. Those whom we have named you here were the richest men [10] and they carried banners,[11] and we have not by any means named all those who carried banners. And of those who did most deeds of prowess and of arms, rich and poor, we can name you a part. Pierre of Bracheux, he was the one among rich and poor who did most deeds of prowess, and Hugh his brother and Andrew of Dureboise and my lord Pierre of Amiens, the worthy and the fair, and Matthew of Montmorency and Matthew of Warlincourt and Baldwin of Beauvoir and Henry, the brother of the count of Flanders, and James of Avesnes. These were those of the rich men who did most deeds of arms. And of the poor, Bernard of Aire and Bernard of Soubrengien, Eustace of Heu-

[8] The "Île de France," the region around Paris. Beauvaisis and Chartrain mean respectively the district of Beauvais and the district of Chartres.

[9] By inadvertence Robert repeats the name of Pierre of Amiens, mentioned earlier among those of Aminois, and goes on to add other names from that region.

[10] *li plus rike homme.* Old French *riche* implies power and importance as well as wealth.

[11] *baniere.* This is one of the very earliest instances of the use of the word "banner" in its technical sense as a standard carried in battle, the right to which was a mark of feudal rank. Guillaume le Breton, who wrote his chronicle just about this time, uses the Latin term *vexillum,* "standard," in this sense (*Œuvres de Rigord et de Guillaume le Breton,* I, 290), and in the contemporary acts of Philip Augustus we find the term *vexillarii,* "knights banneret." See Guilhiermoz, *Essai,* pp. 138-71.

mont and his brother, Gilbert of Vismes, Wales of Frise, Hugh of Beauvais, Robert of Ronsoi, Alard Maquereau, Nicholas of Mailly, Guy of Manchecourt, Baldwin of Hamelincourt, William of Embreville, Aleaumes of Clari in Aminois, the clerk, who was right worthy and did many deeds of hardihood and of prowess there, Aleaumes of Sains [and] Willerames of Fontaine. Those whom we have named here were those who did most deeds of arms and of prowess there. And many other good people, on horse and on foot, so many thousands that we do not know the number of them.

Then there came together all the counts and the high barons who had taken the cross. And they sent for all the high men who had taken the cross, and when they were all come together, they took counsel among them as to whom they should make their chieftain and lord, until they took Count Thibaut of Champagne and made him their lord. Then they parted from one another and went away each to his own country. And then it was not a great while afterwards that Count Thibaut died, and he left fifty thousand livres to the crusaders and to the one who after him should be chieftain and lord of the crusaders and to do with as the crusaders should wish. And Master Fulk died also, which was a very great loss to the crusaders.[12]

When the crusaders knew that the count of Champagne, their lord, was dead, and Master Fulk also, they were very sad and greatly troubled and greatly dismayed. And they all came together on a certain day at Soissons and took counsel among them as to what they should do and whom they should make their chieftain and lord, and finally they agreed among them to send for the marquis of Montferrat in Lombardy.[13] They sent right

---

[12] Count Thibaut died in May, 1201, and Fulk just a year later in May, 1202. The death of Fulk is in the wrong place in the narrative, since it occurred some time after the election of the marquis.

[13] The marquis Boniface. This powerful family of Lombardy was connected by marriage both with the Capetians and with the Hohenstaufen, and its members had played important rôles in the kingdom of Jerusalem and in the Byzantine empire. The father, William the Old, had gone on the Second Crusade and had spent some time in the Holy Land. Returning later, he was captured by Saladin in the fatal battle of Hattin in 1187.

good messengers for him there. The messengers got them ready and went to the marquis. When they came there, they spoke to the marquis and said to him that the barons of France greeted him and sent word to him to pray him in God's name to come and talk with them on a certain day, which they named to him. When the marquis heard this, he wondered much that the barons of France should have sent for him, and he answered the messengers that he would take thought on it and let them know on the morrow what he would do about it. And he did great honor to the messengers.[14] When the morrow was come, the marquis said to them that he would go to talk with them at Soissons on the day they had named to him. Then the messengers took their leave and went back, and the marquis offered them some of his horses and jewels, but they would not take any of them. When they were returned, they made known to the barons what they had done. Then the marquis got ready his gear and crossed over Mont Joux and went on into France to Soissons. And he made known to the barons in advance that he was coming and the barons were there to meet him and did him great honor.

When the marquis was come to Soissons, he asked the barons why they had sent for him. Now the barons had taken counsel together, and they said to him: "Sir, we have sent for you because the count of Champagne, our lord, who was our commander, is dead. So we sent for you as the most worthy man that we knew, and the one who, God willing, could give us the best counsel in our affair. And we all pray you, in God's name, to be our lord and to take the cross for the love of God." With these words, the barons kneeled down before him. And

---

Boniface's oldest brother, William Longsword, married Sibylle of Jerusalem and was the father of Baldwin V. The next oldest brother was the famous Conrad of Montferrat. He married Isabelle of Jerusalem and was recognized as king in 1192, but was assassinated the same year. His exploits at Constantinople and at Tyre are narrated by Robert later on. A younger brother, Rainer, married a daughter of Emperor Manuel of Constantinople and perished in the palace revolution of 1183. See Ilgen, *Markgraf Conrad von Montferrat.*

[14] *fist molt feste des messages;* this expression recurs frequently.

they said he should not be dismayed at undertaking it, for they would give him a large part of the money which the count of Champagne had left to the crusaders. The marquis said that he would think on it, and when he had done so, he answered that he would take the cross, for the love of God and in order to succor the land oversea. Then the bishop of Soissons was straightway vested, and he gave the marquis the cross; and when he had taken the cross they gave him twenty-five thousand livres out of the money which the count of Champagne had left to the crusaders.

Afterwards, when the marquis had taken the cross, he said to the barons: "Lords," said the marquis, "where will you want to pass oversea, and to what land of the Saracens will you want to go?" The barons answered that they did not want to go to the land of Syria, for they would not be able to accomplish anything there, but they had thought of going to Babylon[15] or to Alexandria, there in the very midst of things, where they would be able to do most, and had planned to hire a fleet which could transport them there all together. Then the marquis said that this was a good plan and he was right well agreed to it, and that they should send good messengers from among their best knights to Pisa or Genoa or Venice. To this plan the barons all agreed.

Then they chose their messengers, and they all agreed that Conon of Béthune should go and the marshal of Champagne.[16] Then when they had chosen their messengers, the barons parted from one another, and the marquis went away to his own coun-

[15] The common name in the West for Cairo; so used in the *Anonymi gesta*, Fulcher of Chartres, William of Tyre, etc. Miss Lees, in her edition of the *Anonymi gesta* (p. 117), says: "The name Babylon, strictly speaking, refers to the old fortress at some distance from the modern Cairo, which is said to have been built by one of the later Pharaohs to receive the Babylonian mercenaries in the Egyptian service."

[16] Villehardouin (§ 12) gives the correct list, which is also found in the texts of the treaties (Tafel and Thomas, I, 362 ff.): the envoys of Count Thibaut were Geoffrey of Villehardouin and Miles of Brabant; of Count Baldwin, Conon of Béthune and Alard Maquereau; of Count Louis, John of Friaise and Walter of Gaudonville.

try and each of the others likewise. They commanded the messengers to hire vessels to transport four thousand knights and their harness and one hundred thousand men on foot. The messengers got ready their gear and went straight on until they came to Genoa, and they spoke to the Genoese and told them what they were seeking, and the Genoese said they could not help them in it at all. Then they went to Pisa and spoke to them of Pisa, and they answered them that they did not have so many vessels and could not do anything for them. Then they went on to Venice and spoke to the doge of Venice and told him what they were seeking: that they wanted to hire passage for four thousand knights and their harness and for one hundred thousand men on foot. When the doge heard of this, he said he would think on it, for so great an affair ought to be well considered. Then the doge summoned all the high councilors of the city and spoke to them and showed them what had been asked of him. And when they had counseled together the doge answered the messengers and said to them: "Lords, we are willing to make a bargain with you. We will find you a navy large enough for your needs for one hundred thousand marks, if you agree, on the understanding that I shall go along with half of those who are able to bear arms from all of Venice and that we shall have half of all the gains that are made there. And we will add fifty galleys at our own cost. And within a year from the day we shall name we will set you in whatever land you wish, whether at Babylon or at Alexandria." When the messengers heard this, they replied that a hundred thousand marks would be too much, and they talked together until they made a bargain for eighty and seven thousand marks, and the doge and the Venetians and the messengers swore to keep this bargain. Then the doge said that he wanted to have twenty-five thousand marks as advance payment, in order to begin building the navy. The messengers replied that he should send messengers back with them to France, and they would gladly see to it that the twenty-five thousand marks were paid to them. Then the messengers took leave and went on back, and the doge sent a high man of Venice along with them to receive the advance payment.[17]

Then the doge had his ban cried through all Venice, that no Venetian should be so bold as to engage in any business, but rather they should all help to build the navy, and they did so. So they began to build the richest navy that ever was seen.

When the messengers came to France, they made it known that they were come. Then word was sent to all the barons who had taken the cross that they were to come straightway to Corbie. When they were all come together, the messengers told what they had done. When the barons heard it, they were greatly pleased and they approved right well what they had done. And they did great honor to the messengers of the doge of Venice, and they gave them some of the money left by the count of Champagne and some of the money which Master Fulk had collected, and the count of Flanders put in some of his money, until there were twenty-five thousand marks. So they gave this money to the messenger [18] of the doge of Venice and they gave him safe-conduct to go with it to his own country.

Then word was sent to all the crusaders through all the lands, that they should all set out at Easter to go to Venice,

[17] The actual treaties between the doge of Venice on the one side and the envoys of the three counts of Champagne, Flanders, and Blois on the other are found in Tafel and Thomas (I, 362 ff.). The terms were as follows: the service for a year of a fleet large enough to transport 4,500 knights and their horses, 9,000 squires, and 20,000 foot soldiers, together with their arms and armor and provisions. In addition, the doge promised fifty armed galleys, also for a year's service. The year was to be reckoned from the next feast of SS. Peter and Paul (June 29), unless changed by common agreement. For this the crusaders were to pay 85,000 marks of pure silver of the weight of Cologne—15,000 by the first of the next August (1201), 10,000 more by the Feast of All Saints (November 1), 10,000 more by the Purification of the Blessed Virgin (February 20, 1202), and the remaining 50,000 by the end of April. The mark was a money of reckoning, equivalent, at least in the fourteenth century, to about 234 grams of silver, or about the silver of nine silver dollars. Purchasing power, of course, was many times that of the same weight of silver today. Villehardouin, one of the negotiators of the agreement, gives the correct terms (§§ 20 ff.), but he does not mention any dispute about the price.

[18] This confusion between singular and plural is found in the manuscript.

so as to be there between Pentecost and August, without fail,
and they did so. So when Easter was past they all came together. Many there were of fathers and mothers, sisters and
brothers, wives and children, who made great lamenting over
their loved ones.

When the pilgrims were all assembled at Venice and saw
the rich navy that had been made, the rich ships, the great
freighters,[19] the transports [20] to carry the horses, and the
galleys, they marveled at it greatly and at the great riches
which they found in the city. When they saw that they could
not all find quarters in the city, they decided among them to
go and quarter themselves on the Isle of St. Nicholas,[21] which
was entirely surrounded by sea and was a league away from
Venice. So the pilgrims went there and set up their tents and
quartered themselves the best they could.

When the doge of Venice saw that all the pilgrims were
come, he sent for all those of his land of Venice. And when
they were all come, the doge commanded that half of them
should equip themselves and make ready to go along in the
fleet with the pilgrims. When the Venetians heard this, some
of them were glad, but others said they could not go; and
they were not able to decide how the half of them should be
chosen to go. Finally they made a drawing of lots in this way:
balls of wax were made in pairs and in one of the two they
put a slip of paper. Then they came to the priest and gave

[19] *dromons*. This term is rather rare in the West, except in poetry; the
Estoire de la guerre sainte uses it in describing the fleet of Richard Lionheart. It was originally applied by the Byzantine Greeks to the fast war
galley, but by this time it had come to mean the great freighter. It is so
used by William of Tyre in describing the fleet brought together by Emperor
Manuel for the attack on Egypt in 1169, and by Ralph of Coggeshall, *anno*
1191, in describing the great Saracen ship encountered by the English fleet
on the way to Acre.
[20] *uissiers*, so called from the door or port (*huis*) in the side of the vessel
for the loading and unloading of the horses. See note on the fleet and the
forces, p. 132.
[21] The present Lido. The medieval name was taken from the church of
St. Nicholas on the island, to which the relics of the saint had been brought
in 1100.

them to him and he made the sign of the cross over them and gave one of the two balls to each of two Venetians and the one who had the ball with the writing in it had to go with the fleet. So they were divided. Now when the pilgrims had taken quarters on the Isle of St. Nicholas, the doge of Venice and the Venetians went to talk with them, and they demanded their pay for the navy which they had prepared. And the doge said to them that they had done ill in this, that they had sent word by their messengers to have a navy prepared for four thousand knights and their harness and for one hundred thousand men on foot, and of these four thousand knights there were not more than a thousand, because some had gone to other ports, and of these hundred thousand men on foot there were not more than fifty thousand or sixty. "So," said the doge, "we want you to pay us the covenanted price that was agreed on between us." When the crusaders heard this, they talked together and agreed among them that each knight should give four marks and each horse four [*sic*] and each mounted sergeant two, and that he who gave less should give at least one mark. When they had gathered this money, they gave it to the Venetians and there still remained fifty thousand marks to pay. When the doge and the Venetians saw that the pilgrims had not paid them more than this, they were all very angry. Finally the doge said to them: "Lords," said he, "you have used us ill, for as soon as your messengers had made the bargain with me I commanded through all my land that no trader should go a-trading, but that all should help prepare this navy. So they have waited ever since and have not made any money for a year and a half past. Instead, they have lost a great deal, and therefore we wish, my men and I, that you should pay us the money you owe us. And if you do not do so, then know that you shall not depart from this island before we are paid, nor shall you find anyone to bring you anything to eat or to drink." The doge was a right worthy man, and so he did not cease from having brought to them enough to eat and to drink.[22]

[22] *si ne laissa mie pour chou que on ne leur portast asses a boire et a menger.* In other places in the manuscript we find confusion between *laissa*, "per-

When the counts and the crusaders heard what the doge said, they were sorely grieved and greatly dismayed. Then they made another collection and borrowed as much money as they could from those who they thought had any, and they paid this to the Venetians, and when they had paid it, there still remained thirty-six thousand marks to pay. And they told them that they were in an evil plight and that the host was impoverished by this collection which they had made and that they could not raise any more money to pay them, but rather had scarcely enough for the host to live on. When the doge saw that they could not pay all the money, but were indeed in very hard straits because of it, he spoke to his own people and said: "Lords," said he, "if we let these men go back to their own land, we shall always be held for rogues and cheats. Rather let us go to them and tell them that if they will pay us the thirty-six thousand marks they owe us, out of the first gains which they shall make for themselves, we will put them overseas." The Venetians agreed willingly to what the doge said. So they went to the pilgrims where they were quartered, and when they were come there the doge said to them: "Lords," said he, "we have taken counsel, I and my people, to this effect, that if you are willing to promise faithfully to pay us the thirty-six thousand marks you owe us, out of the first gains that you shall make for yourselves, we will put you oversea." When the crusaders heard what the doge said and proposed, they were right glad, and they fell at his feet for joy and promised faithfully that they would do what the doge had devised. And there was such rejoicing that night that there was no one so poor as not to make a great illumination, and they carried great torches on the end of their lances around their lodges and inside of them, so that it seemed as if the whole camp were on fire.

---

mitted," and *lassa*, "ceased, gave over," so that this passage may have either the meaning given above in the translation, or the opposite: "nevertheless, he did not allow them to bring them enough to eat and to drink." The *Devastatio*, which is hostile to the Venetians, says that the crusaders were kept on the island as virtual prisoners and suffered heavy losses.

Afterwards the doge came to them and said: "Lords, it is now winter and we cannot cross oversea. The fault cannot be laid on me, for I would have had you make the crossing long ago if it had not been for you. But let us make the best of it," said the doge. "There is a city near here, Zara[23] is its name. They of the city have done us much harm, and I and my men want to be avenged on them if we can. If you will trust me, we will go there and stay there this winter until toward Easter, and then we will make ready our fleet and go oversea to the service of God. For Zara is a very fine city and plenteous in all good things." The barons and the high men of the crusaders agreed to what the doge had said, but the host as a whole did not know anything of this plan, save only the highest men. Then they all got ready their gear and their navy and put to sea. And each of the high men had his own ship for himself and his people, and his transport to carry his horses, and the doge had with him fifty galleys all at his own cost. The galley he was in was all vermilion and it had a canopy of vermilion samite spread over him, and there were four silver trumpets trumpeting before him and drums making a great noise. And all the high men, and the clerks and laymen, and great and small, displayed so much joy at the departure that never yet was there such rejoicing, nor was ever such a fleet seen or heard of. And the pilgrims had all the priests and clerks mount on the high poops of the ships to chant the *Veni creator spiritus.* And everyone, great and small, wept with emotion and for the great joy they had. When the fleet set out from the harbor of Venice . . .[24] freighters and these rich ships and so many other vessels, that it was the finest thing to see that has ever been since the beginning of the world. For there were fully a hundred pairs of trumpets, of silver and of brass, all sounding at the departure, and so many drums and tabors and other instruments that it was a fair marvel. When they were on that sea and had spread their sails and had their banners set high

---

[23] *Jadres*, the usual medieval name. In 1181 Zara had expelled its Venetian governor and submitted itself to Bela III, king of Hungary.

[24] A half-line blank in the manuscript.

on the poops of the ships and their ensigns, it seemed indeed as if the sea were all a-tremble and all on fire with the ships they were sailing and the great joy they were making. Then they went on until they came to a city, Pola was its name. There they made land and refreshed themselves and stayed there a little, until they were well restored and had bought new provisions to put in their ships. Afterwards they put to sea again. And if they had made much joy and festivity before, now they made as much or even more, so that the people of the city were amazed at the great joy and at the mighty fleet and at the noble display they made. And they said, and it was true, that never had so fair a fleet or so rich been seen or assembled in any land as there was there.

The Venetians and the pilgrims sailed until they came to Zara on the eve of the feast of St. Martin.[25] Now they of the city of Zara were sore afraid when they saw these ships and this mighty fleet approaching, so they had the gates of the city closed and took arms to defend themselves as best they could. When they were armed, the doge spoke to all the high men of the host and said to them: "Lords, this city has done much harm to me and to my people, and I would gladly avenge myself on it. So I pray you to help me." And the barons and the high men answered that they would gladly help him. Now the people of Zara knew right well that the Venetians hated them, so they had secured a letter from Rome, saying that anyone who should make war on them or do them any harm would be excommunicated.[26] And they sent this letter by good mes-

[25] St. Martin's day is November 11. The month between the departure from Venice, October 9, and the arrival before Zara is accounted for by the actions of the fleet. According to the chronicle of Dandulo, the doge went with a part of the fleet to secure the submission of Trieste and Moglie. The treaties with these towns are published in Tafel and Thomas, I, 386 f., 396 f.

[26] The policy of Innocent III in the matter of Zara is rather obscure. The best account is found in Luchaire, *Innocent III: la question d'Orient*, pp. 98 ff. Villehardouin seems to have suppressed some of the facts. The story is told from various angles in the *Gesta Innocentii*, the letters of Innocent, the Anonymous of Halberstadt, Gunther of Pairis, the *Hystoria albigensis* of Pierre of Vaux-de-Cernay, and the *Devastatio*.

sengers to the doge and the pilgrims who had landed there. When the messengers came to the camp, the letter was read before the doge and the pilgrims, and when the letter was read and the doge had heard it, he said that he would not give over having his revenge on those of the city, not even for the excommunication of the apostolic. At that the messengers went away. Then the doge spoke again to the barons and said: "Lords, know you well that I will not in any degree give over being avenged on them, no, not even for the apostolic." And he prayed the barons to help him. The barons all answered that they would gladly help him, save only Count Simon of Montfort and my lord Enguerrand of Boves. These said that they would not go against the commandments of the apostolic, nor did they want to be excommunicated. So they made themselves ready and went to Hungary to stay there all the winter.[27] When the doge saw that the barons would help him, he had his engines set up to assault the city, until they of the city saw that they could not long hold out. So they threw themselves on their mercy and surrendered the city to them. Then the pilgrims and the Venetians entered in, and the city was divided into two halves so that the pilgrims had one half and the Venetians the other.[28]

Afterwards it happened that a great fray arose between the Venetians and the common people of the pilgrims, which lasted fully a night and half a day, and this fray was so fierce that the knights were scarcely able to part them. When they had parted them, they made so good a peace that never afterwards was there ill-will between them. Then the high men of the

[27] The *Hystoria albigensis* has a vivid account of the violent scene between the doge and Simon de Montfort on the occasion when the abbot of Vaux-de-Cernay read the papal warning. According to this chronicle, the author of which was a nephew of the abbot, Simon withdrew from the camp and left to go to Barletta in Apulia and there take ship for the Holy Land. Villehardouin and Ernoul agree with Robert in saying that Simon went to Hungary and from there to the Holy Land.

[28] Dandulo relates the later fate of the city of Zara, how it revolted again and was finally reduced to subjection by the doge's son, Reiner, in 1203. The final treaty is found in Tafel and Thomas, II, 421 ff.

crusaders and the Venetians talked together about the excommunication that had been laid upon them because of the city which they had taken, until they agreed together to send to Rome to be absolved. So they sent the bishop of Soissons and my lord Robert of Boves,[29] and these men procured a letter from the apostolic that all the pilgrims and all the Venetians were absolved. When they had their letter, the bishop returned as soon as he could, but my lord Robert of Boves did not return with him; instead he went oversea straight from Rome.

In the meantime, while the crusaders and the Venetians were staying there that winter, the crusaders bethought them that they had spent a great deal. And they talked with one another and said that they could not go to Babylon or to Alexandria or to Syria, because they had neither provisions nor money for going there. For they had spent nearly everything, on the long delay they had made as well as on the great price they had given for the hire of the fleet. So they said they could not go, and if they went they would not be able to do anything, because they had neither money nor provisions to maintain themselves.

The doge of Venice saw right well that the pilgrims were in sore straits, and he spoke to them and said: "Lords, in Greece there is a land that is very rich and plenteous in all good things. If we could have a reasonable excuse [30] for going there and taking provisions and other things in the land until we were well restored, it would seem to me a good plan. Then we should be well able to go oversea." Then the marquis rose and said: "Lords, last year at Christmas I was in Germany at the court of my lord the emperor. There I saw a youth who was

---

[29] According to Villehardouin, the crusaders chose two of the clergy, the bishop of Soissons and John of Noyon, and two lords, John of Friaise and Robert of Boves. Gunther of Pairis says that his abbot was also a member of the embassy. Robert is in error in saying that the Venetians associated themselves with the crusaders in the request for absolution.

[30] Pope Innocent had warned the crusaders not to attack any Christian lands "unless the inhabitants should wickedly oppose their march or some other *just or necessary cause* should arise." See the letter in Migne, *Pat. Lat.*, CCXIV, col. 1178.

brother to the wife of the emperor of Germany.[31] This youth
was the son of the emperor Isaac[32] of Constantinople, whose
brother had taken the empire of Constantinople from him by
treason. Whoever could get hold of this youth," said the
marquis, "would be well able to go to Constantinople and get
provisions and other things, for this youth is the rightful
heir." [33]

Now we shall leave off here about the pilgrims and the
fleet,[34] and we shall tell you about this youth and the emperor
Isaac, his father, how they arose. There was once an emperor
in Constantinople, Manuel was his name.[35] This emperor was
a right worthy man and the richest of all Christians who have
ever been, and the most generous. Never did anyone ask him
for anything of his—anyone who was of the law of Rome and
who was able to speak to him—but that he would give him a
hundred marks; so, at least, we have heard it told. This emperor loved the French very much and much he trusted them.
Now it happened one day that the people of his land and his
councilors reproached him greatly, as they had many times
before reproached him, for being so generous and for loving
the French so much. And the emperor answered them: "There
are only two who have the right to give, the Lord God and I.

[31] Alexius, later Alexius IV Angelus, 1203-4. He was the son of Isaac
and a former wife and is said to have been twelve years old in 1195, when
his father was blinded and deposed. His sister Irene was married to Philip of
Swabia.

[32] *Kyrsac.* This is Isaac II Angelus, 1185-95. The Greek honorary title,
Kurios Isaak, Kur' Isaak, "Lord Isaac," gave rise to the various forms of
the name by which he was known in Western chronicles: Kyr Ysac, Kirsac,
Kirisacus, Tursachus, etc.

[33] The chronology of the flight and journeyings of young Alexius is a
central element in the "diversion question" and has been discussed by the
scholars who have struggled with that question (see note 25, Introduction).
According to Villehardouin, however, young Alexius was in northern Italy
on his way to the court of Philip of Swabia in the summer of 1202, so
that the marquis could not have met him there at Christmas, 1201.

[34] *Or vous lairons chi ester des pelerins et de l'estoire:* literally, "Now
we shall let you rest (or stand) here about the pilgrims," etc. This is
Robert's regular locution for a transition.

[35] Manuel I Comnenus, 1143-80.

Nevertheless, if you want me to, I will dismiss the French and all those of the law of Rome who are about me and in my service." And the Greeks were very glad of this and said: "Ah, sire! then you will do a very good thing, and we will serve you right well for it." So the emperor commanded all the French to go away, and the Greeks were glad of it more than a great deal. Then the emperor sent word to all the Frenchmen and all the others whom he had dismissed from his service to come and talk with him privily, and they did so. When they were come, the emperor said to them: "Lords, my people give me no peace, telling me not to give you anything and to hunt you out of my land. But now do you all go away together, and I will follow you, I and my people. And you will be in a certain place," and he named it to them, "and I will send word to you by my messengers to go away. Then you will send back word to me that you will not go away, not for me nor for all my people. Instead, you will make a great show of coming at me. Then I shall see how my people will prove themselves." And they did so straightway. Now when they were gone, the emperor sent for all his people and followed them. And when he came near to them, he sent them word to go away forthwith and vacate his land, and those who had advised the emperor to hunt them out of his land were greatly pleased and they said to the emperor: "Sire, if they will not go forthwith, give us leave to slay them all." And the emperor answered: "Willingly." When the messengers of the emperor came to the French, they delivered their message very haughtily, that they should go away forthwith. The French answered the messengers and said that they would not go away, not for the emperor nor for all his people. Then the messengers came back and told what the French had answered, and the emperor commanded his people to arm themselves and help him attack the French. And they all armed themselves and advanced toward the French. And the French came to meet them and they had their battles [36] well ordered. When the emperor saw that they were coming toward him and his people

[36] *batailles*, battalions, combat divisions.

to fight with them, he said to his people: "Lords, now bethink you to acquit yourselves well. Now you can have your revenge on them." As he said this, the Greeks were taken with a great fear of the Latins—for they call all those of the law of Rome, Latins—whom they saw approaching. And the Latins made a great show of riding at them. When the Greeks saw this, they turned to flee and left the emperor all alone. When the emperor saw this, he said to the French: "Lords, come back now with me, and I will give you more than I have ever yet done." So he brought the French back with him. When he was returned, he summoned his people and said to them: "Lords, now it can well be seen who is to be trusted. You fled away when you should have helped me and you left me all alone, and if the Latins had wanted to they could have cut me to pieces. So now I command that no one of you be so bold or so hardy as ever to speak again about my largesse or about my loving the French. For I do love them and put my trust in them more than I do in you, and I shall give them more than I have ever given them before." And the Greeks were never again so bold as to dare to speak to him about it.

This emperor Manuel had a very fine son [37] by his wife, and he bethought himself that he would like to make for him the highest marriage that he could. So on the advice of the French who were about him he sent word to Philip, king of France, to give him his sister for his son. So the emperor sent to France messengers who were very high men and who went in very rich array. Never were people seen to go more richly or more nobly than these did, so that the king of France and his people marveled greatly at the noble display the messengers made. When the messengers came to the king, they told him what the emperor wanted of him, and the king said he would take counsel on it. And when he had taken counsel his barons advised him to send his sister to a man as high and as rich as the emperor

[37] The child emperor, Alexius II, 1180-83. He was married to Agnes, the daughter of Louis VII and Alix of Champagne and the own sister of Philip Augustus. She was then some ten or twelve years old. As empress she was given the Greek name Anna.

was. Then the king answered the messengers that he would gladly send his sister to the emperor.

Then the king arrayed his sister very richly and sent her with the messengers to Constantinople, and many of his people with her. And they rode and journeyed without stopping until they came to Constantinople. When they were come, the emperor did very great honor to the damsel and made great rejoicing over her and her people. In the meantime, while the emperor was sending for this damsel, he also sent one of his kinsmen, whom he loved very much, Andronicus [38] was his name, in the other direction oversea for the queen Theodora [39] of Jerusalem, who was his sister, so that she might come to the coronation of his son and to his wedding feast. So the queen put to sea with Andronicus to come to Constantinople. When they were well out to sea, what does Andronicus do but become enamored of the queen, [40] who was his cousin, and he lay with her by force. And when he had done this, he dared not return to Constantinople, but he took the queen and carried her off by force to Konia [41] among the Saracens, and there he stayed.

When the emperor Manuel heard the news that Andronicus had thus carried off the queen, his sister, he was greatly grieved, but he did not for that give over making a great feast and crowning his son and the damsel. And it was not long afterwards that the emperor died. When Andronicus the traitor heard it told that the emperor Manuel was dead, he sent to his son who was now emperor to beseech him in God's name to lay aside his wrath. And he made him believe that it was nothing but a lie that had been put upon him, until the emperor,

[38] *Andromes,* Andronicus Comnenus, grandson of Alexius I and cousin-german of Manuel; he was emperor, 1183-85. The life of this extraordinary person is related by Diehl in his *Figures byzantines,* II, 86-133.

[39] *Teudore.* This was Theodora, daughter of Isaac, an older brother of Manuel, therefore Manuel's niece and not his sister. She was the widow of Baldwin III, king of Jerusalem, who had died in 1162.

[40] *si ne fait mais el Andromes si aama le roine:* "Andromes does nothing else (*el*) but loved the queen." This is one of Robert's favorite locutions, which he uses over and over from this point on.

[41] *Coine;* ancient Iconium.

who was only a child, laid aside his wrath and sent for him. So this Andronicus came back and was always in the company of the child, and the child made him steward of all his land, and he became more than a little haughty over the stewardship which he held. And it was not a great while after that that he took the emperor by night and murdered him and his mother also. When he had done this, he took two great stones and had them tied to their necks and then had them thrown into the sea. Then he had himself straightway crowned emperor by force. When he was crowned, he had all those seized who he knew bore it ill that he was emperor, and he had their eyes put out and had them slain and made to die shameful deaths. And he took all the beautiful women he found and lay with them by force. And he took to wife the empress who was sister to the king of France, and he did so many great villainies that never did any traitor or murderer do as many as he did. When he had done all these villainies, then he asked a chief steward of his, who helped him do all these evil deeds, if there were any left of those who bore it ill that he was emperor. And he answered that he did not know of any, save that it was said that there were three young men in the city who were of the lineage called the lineage of the Angeli,[42] and they were high men, but they were not rich; instead they were poor and did not have any great power. When the emperor Andronicus heard that these three youths were indeed of this lineage, he commanded this steward of his, who was a right wicked man and as great a traitor as he was himself, to go and take them and hang them or make them die some evil death. The steward went off to take these three brothers, but he took only one of them and the other two escaped. The one who was taken had his eyes put out and afterwards he became a monk. The other two fled, and one of them went to a land called Vlachia.[43] This one was

[42] This family was descended from one Constantine Angelus who married a daughter of the emperor Alexius I.

[43] *Blakie.* The territory occupied by the Vlachs, including part of Thessaly and part of Epirus, was known to the Greeks as "great Blachia" (Nicetas, p. 841). The name survives in modern Walachia.

named Isaac. And the other went away to Antioch and was captured by the Saracens during a raid made by the Christians. The one who fled to Vlachia was so poor that he could not maintain himself, so that he came back to Constantinople for very poverty. And he concealed himself in the house of a widowed woman in the city. Now he had no chattels in the world except a mule and one servant. This servant earned wages with his mule by carrying wine and other things, whereby Isaac, his master, and he managed to live. Finally the news came to the emperor Andronicus, the traitor, that this youth had in fact returned to the city. Then he commanded his steward, who was greatly hated by all the people for the evil that he did every day, to go and take this Isaac and hang him. So one day the steward mounted his horse and took many people with him and went to the house of the good woman where Isaac was staying. When he came there, he made them call at the door, and the good woman came out, wondering greatly what he wanted, until he ordered her to make him who was concealed in the house come out. The good woman answered and said, "Ah, sire! by God's mercy, there is no one hidden within." Then he commanded her again to make him come out, or if she did not make him come he would have them both seized. When the good woman heard this, she had great fear of this devil who had done so much evil, and she went into the house and came to the youth and said to him: "Ah, fair lord Isaac! you are a dead man. Here is the emperor's steward and many people with him, who are come seeking you to destroy and to slay you." The youth was sore dismayed when he heard this news; nevertheless he came, since there was no way to avoid going out to meet the steward. So what does he do but take his sword and put it under his coat and come out from the house. And he came up to the steward and said to him: "Sir, what do you want?" And he answered him right villainously and said: "Stinking wretch, now they are going to hang you." So Isaac saw that he would have to go with them in spite of himself, and he would gladly have avenged himself on some of them. So he came as close to the steward as he could and

drew his sword and struck the steward in the middle of his
head and clove him through clear to the teeth.

When the sergeants and the people who were with the
steward saw that the youth had thus cut down the steward,
they fled away. And when the youth saw that they were fleeing
away, he seized the horse of the steward whom he had slain
and mounted it, and he still held his sword which was dripping
with blood. And what did he do but set out to go toward the
church of Saint Sophia, and as he went along he kept calling
for mercy to the people who were thronging the streets, all
in a maze at the tumult they had heard. And the youth called
out to them: "Lords, for the mercy of God, do not kill me,
for I have slain the devil and murderer who has done so much
shame to those of this city and to others." When he was come
to the church of Saint Sophia, he went up to the altar and
embraced the cross, because he wanted to save his life. Then
the noise and the tumult were loud in the city, and the cry
went up and down until it was known through all the city that
Isaac had slain that demon and murderer. When they of the
city knew it, they were right glad of it, and they ran each as
best he could to the church of Saint Sophia to see the youth
that had done this hardihood. And when they were all assembled there, they began to say to one another: "He is valiant
and brave, since he dared to do this great hardihood." Finally
the Greeks said among them: "Let us do the right thing. Let
us make this youth the emperor." And in the end they were
all of one accord. So they sent for the patriarch, who was right
there in his palace, to come and crown a new emperor whom they
had chosen. When the patriarch heard this, he said he would
not do anything of the sort, and he began to say to them:
"Lords, you are doing ill. Calm yourselves. You are not doing
right to undertake such a thing. If I were to crown him, the
emperor Andronicus would slay me and cut me to pieces."
And the Greeks answered that if he did not crown him they
would cut off his head. So the patriarch, perforce and for the
fear that he had, came down from his palace and went to
the church, there where Isaac was in a wretched cloak and in

wretched garments, he for whom that very day the emperor Andronicus had sent his steward and people to take and destroy him. So the patriarch, whether he would or no, vested himself and crowned him there forthwith. When Isaac was crowned, the news of it went up and down, until Andronicus heard of it and learned too that he had slain his steward. And he could never believe it until he sent his messengers there, and when his messengers came there, they saw that it was indeed true. So they came back straightway to the emperor and said: "Sire, it is all true."

When the emperor knew that it was true, he rose and took many of his people with him and went to the church of Saint Sophia by a passage that led from his palace to the church.[44] When he came to the church, he got himself up on the vaults of the church [45] and saw him who had been crowned. When he saw him, he was very angry and he asked his people if there was anyone of them that had a bow, and they brought him a bow and arrow. And Andronicus took the bow and bent it and made to shoot Isaac, who had been crowned, through the body. And as he bent the bow, the cord broke, and he was sore dismayed and in great despair. Then he went back to the palace and told his people to go and shut the gates and arm themselves to defend the palace, and they did so. In the meantime, he left the palace and came to a secret postern and went out of the city and entered into a galley, and some of his people with him. And they put to sea, because he did not want the people of the city to take him.

Then the people of the city went to the palace and took the new emperor with them. And they seized the palace by force and led the emperor into it. Then they seated him on the throne of Constantine, and then when he was seated on the throne of Constantine they all adored him as the holy emperor.

[44] Andronicus occupied the Great Palace (which Robert calls *Bouke de Lion*), close to Saint Sophia. Ebersolt (*Le Grand Palais*, p. 25, note 1) speaks of a passage by which one could go from the Chalké, or great entrance hall of the palace, to the upper galleries of Saint Sophia.

[45] The gallery supported by the vaults over the aisle.

The emperor was very happy over the great honor that God had given him that day, and he said to the people: "Lords, now see the marvel of the great honor that God has given me, that on the very day on which they were going to take and slay me, on that very day I am crowned emperor. And for the great honor that you have done me, I give you now all the treasure that is in this palace and in the palace of Blachernae." [46] When the people heard this, they were very glad of the great gift which the emperor had given them, and they went and broke into the treasure and they found there so much gold and silver that it was a fair marvel, and they divided it up among them.

The same night on which Andronicus fled, there arose so great a storm at sea and so great a tempest of wind and thunder and lightning that he and his people knew not where they were going. And finally the storm and the tempest drove them back to Constantinople without their knowing it. When they saw that they were driven on shore and could not go on, Andronicus said to his people: "Lords, see where we are." They looked and saw right well that they were come back to Constantinople, and they said to Andronicus: "Sire, we are dead men, for we are come back to Constantinople." When Andronicus heard this, he was so dismayed that he knew not what to do. And he said to his people: "Lords, for God's sake, take us somewhere away from here." And they answered that they could not go on, were he to cut off their heads. When they saw that they could not go any farther, they took Andronicus the emperor and led him to an inn and hid him behind the wine casks. The innkeeper and his wife looked right well at these people and they were well aware that they were the people of the emperor Andronicus. And finally the wife of the innkeeper happened to go among the casks to see if they were all secured, and she looked around and saw Andronicus

---

[46] The palace of Blachernae was at the other end of the city in the corner made by the land walls and the Golden Horn; see map, facing p. 31: D. This had been the favorite residence of the emperors from Alexius I to Manuel I. Andronicus, as we have seen, occupied the Great Palace.

sitting behind the casks in all his imperial robes, and she recognized him right well. So she went back to her husband and said to him: "Sir, Andronicus the emperor is hidden within there." When the innkeeper heard it, he sent a messenger to a certain high man who lived near by in a large palace, whose father Andronicus had slain. And he had lain by force with the wife of this high man. When the messenger came there, he said to this high man that Andronicus was at the house of an innkeeper, and he named him. When the high man heard that Andronicus was at the house of this innkeeper, he was very glad of it and he went with some of his people to the house of the innkeeper and took Andronicus and led him away to his palace. And when morning was come on the morrow, the high man took Andronicus and led him to the palace before the emperor Isaac. When Isaac saw him, he asked him: "Andronicus, why didst thou thus betray thy lord, the emperor Manuel, and why didst thou murder his wife and his son, and why didst thou take delight in doing so much evil to those who bore it ill that thou wert emperor, and why didst thou seek to have me taken?" And Andronicus answered: "Be still," said he, "I would not deign to answer you." When the emperor Isaac heard that he would not deign to answer him, he sent for a great many of those of the city to come before him. When they were come before him, the emperor said to them: "Lords, here is Andronicus, who did so much evil both to you and to others. It seems to me that I can not do justice upon him according to the wishes of all of you, so I hand him over to you to do with him as you will." Then they of the city were very glad, and they took him, and some said to burn him and others to boil him in a cauldron, so that he would live and suffer longer, and others said to drag him through the streets. And they could not agree among them by what death or by what torture they should kill him, until finally there was a wise man who said: "Lords, if you will take my advice, I will show how we can be right well avenged on him. I have a camel at home which is the vilest and most loathsome beast in the world. We will take Andronicus and strip him naked and bind him on the back of the camel, so that his face is right in its rump, and then we will lead him from one end of the city to the other. Then all those, both men and women, to whom he has done evil can be right well revenged on him." And they all agreed to this, and they took Andronicus and bound him as that man had said. And as they led him down through the city, those whom he had wronged came and pierced him and tore him and struck him, some with knives and some with daggers and some with swords. And they said, "You hanged my father"; and, "You lay with my wife by force." And the women whose daughters he had taken by force, they seized him by the beard, and they did him such terrible shame that when they came to the other end of the city there was no flesh left on his bones. Then they took the bones and threw them into a sewer. In such wise did they avenge themselves on this traitor. Now from that day on which Isaac became emperor it was pictured above the portals of the churches how Isaac had become emperor by a miracle, and Our Lord was shown standing on one side of him and Our Lady on the other, placing the crown on his head, and an angel was shown cutting the cord of the bow with which Andronicus wanted to shoot him, wherefore they said his lineage had the name of Angelus.

Afterwards he had a great desire to see his brother who was in captivity in heathendom, so he took messengers and sent them to seek out his brother. They sought until they learned where he was in prison, and they went there. And when they were come there, they asked the Saracens for him. Now the Saracens had heard it said that this youth was the brother of the emperor of Constantinople, and they held him the more dearly for that and said that they would not surrender him without a great price. And finally the messengers gave them as much gold and silver as they demanded. When they had ransomed him, they went back to Constantinople.

When the emperor Isaac saw his brother, he was very glad of it and did him great honor. And that one was very glad also that his brother was emperor and that he had won the empire by his own prowess. This youth was named Alexius.[47] Now it was not long afterwards that the emperor his brother made him steward and high commander of all his land. Then he was made very proud by the stewardship which he held, and the people of the whole empire stood in great awe of him and feared him, because he was brother to the emperor and because the emperor loved him so much.

Afterwards it happened one day that the emperor went hunting in his forest, and what does Alexius his brother do but go into the forest where the emperor was and take him by treason and put out his eyes. Then when he had done this, he had him put in prison in such a way that no one knew anything about it. And when he had done this, he came back to Constantinople and made them believe that the emperor his brother was dead, and he had himself crowned emperor by force. When the governor of the son of the emperor Isaac saw that the uncle of the child had betrayed the child's father and made himself emperor by treason, what does he do but take the boy and send him to Germany, to his sister who was the wife of the emperor of Germany,[48] lest his uncle should have him slain. And he was the more rightful heir than was his uncle Alexius.

Now you have heard how Isaac arose and how he became emperor and how his son went to Germany—he for whom the crusaders and the Venetians were going to send, on the advice of the marquis of Montferrat, their leader, as you have heard before in the story, so that they might have an excuse for going to the country of Constantinople. And now we shall tell you about this youth and the crusaders, how the crusaders sent for him and how they went to Constantinople and how they conquered it.

When the marquis had told the pilgrims and the Venetians that whoever had this youth, of whom we have just spoken, would have a good excuse for going to Constantinople and getting provisions, then the crusaders had two knights right

[47] Alexius III Angelus, emperor 1195-1203.
[48] Irene, daughter of Isaac and wife of Philip of Swabia.

well and finely equipped and sent them to Germany for this youth to come to them. And they sent him word that they would help him gain his rights. When the messengers came to the court of the emperor of Germany, there where the youth was, they told him the message they had been charged to tell. When the youth heard this, and learned the offer which the high men of the crusaders had made to him, he was very glad and made great joy over it. And he was very gracious to the messengers and he said that he would consult with the emperor his brother-in-law. When the emperor heard it, he said to the youth that this was a fine chance that had come to him and that he was greatly in favor of his going to them. And he said that he would never get anything of his heritage unless it should be by the help of God and of the crusaders.

The youth knew well that the emperor was giving him good counsel, and he arrayed himself the finest he could and went off with the messengers. Now before the youth and the messengers were come to Zara, the fleet had gone on to the island of Corfu, because Easter was already past; but when the fleet set out to go there they left two galleys behind to wait for the messengers and the youth.[49] So the pilgrims stayed at the island of Corfu until the youth and the messengers should come. When the youth and the messengers came to Zara, they found these two galleys that had been left for them, and they put to sea and went on until they came to Corfu where the fleet was. When the high men saw the youth coming, they all went to meet him, and they greeted him and did great honor to him, and when the youth saw the high men honoring him so and saw all the fleet that was there, he was glad as no man ever was before. Then the marquis came forward and took the youth and led him away to his tent.

When the youth was there, then all the high barons and the doge of Venice assembled at the tent of the marquis, and they talked of one thing and another, until finally they asked him what he would do for them if they made him em-

---

[49] According to Villehardouin (§§ 110 f.), the marquis and the doge also stayed behind at Zara to wait for Alexius.

peror and made him wear the crown in Constantinople, and he answered them that he would do whatever they wanted. So they parleyed until he said he would give the host two hundred thousand marks and would maintain the fleet a year longer at his own cost and would go oversea with them with all his forces and would keep ten thousand men in the land oversea at his own cost all the days of his life and would give provisions for a whole year to all those who should leave Constantinople to go oversea.[50]

Then all the barons of the host were summoned and the Venetians. And when they were all assembled, the doge of Venice rose and spoke to them. "Lords," said the doge, "now we have a good excuse for going to Constantinople, if you approve of it, for we have the rightful heir." Now there were some who did not at all approve of going to Constantinople. Instead they said: "Bah! what shall we be doing in Constantinople? We have our pilgrimage to make, and also our plan of going to Babylon or Alexandria. Moreover, our navy is to follow us for only a year, and half of the year is already past." And the others said in answer: "What shall we do in Babylon or Alexandria, when we have neither provisions nor money to enable us to go there? Better for us before we go there to secure provisions and money by some good excuse than to go there and die of hunger. Then we shall be able to accomplish something. Moreover, he offers to come with us and to maintain our navy and our fleet a year longer at his own cost." And the marquis of Montferrat was more at pains to urge them to go to Constantinople than anyone else who was there, because he wanted to avenge himself for an injury which the emperor of Constantinople who was then holding the empire had done to him. Now we shall leave off here about the fleet and tell you about the injury for which the marquis hated the emperor of Constantinople. It happened that the marquis Conrad, his brother, took the cross and went oversea and took two galleys with him, and he went by way of Constantinople. And when he

[50] For the terms actually offered by Alexius, see Introduction, p. 13.

came to Constantinople, he spoke to the emperor[51] and the emperor greeted him and gave him good welcome. Now just at that time a high man of the city[52] was besieging the emperor in Constantinople, so that the emperor dared not venture out of the city. When the marquis saw this, he asked the emperor how it was that this man had him so besieged and how it was that he dared not go out and fight with him. The emperor answered that he did not have the heart and the help of his people, and that was why he did not want to fight with him. When the marquis heard this, he said he would help him, if he wanted him to. And the emperor said that he did want it and would be right grateful to him for it. Then the marquis told the emperor to send for all those of the law of Rome, for all the Latins of the city, and he would take them into his company and fight with them to form the vanguard, and the emperor should take all his people with him and follow after him. So the emperor sent for all the Latins of the city, and when they were all come, the emperor commanded them to arm themselves. And when they were all armed and the marquis had made all his own people arm themselves, he took all the Latins with him and ordered his battle the best he could. And the emperor also was fully armed and his people with him. And what does the marquis do but set out in advance,

[51] As noted in the Introduction (p. 20), Robert is here retailing the version of the tale in which the emperor was erroneously supposed to be Alexius III, the one "who was then [1203] holding the empire." In fact, Conrad was in Constantinople in 1187, in the time of Isaac. Nicetas says that Isaac sent envoys to Italy to offer the hand of his sister Theodora to Marquis Boniface. Finding that Boniface was already married, they made the offer to his older brother Conrad, who accepted, came to Constantinople, married Theodora, and received the title of Caesar. After helping Isaac defeat Alexius Branas, he became dissatisfied with his position and prospects in Constantinople, and went to the Holy Land with his followers, where, forgetting his marriage with the Greek princess, he married Isabella, heiress of the kingdom of Jerusalem.

[52] Alexius Branas, whom Robert later calls li Vernas. Some years before he had tried to get the throne by staging a demonstration in Saint Sophia, but this had failed. He was pardoned and put in command of an army to be sent against the Vlachs, but instead of starting on the campaign, he led his army to Constantinople to attack Isaac.

and the emperor follows after him. And as soon as the marquis is outside the gates with all his people, the emperor goes and has the gates closed after him. As soon as Branas, the one who had been besieging the emperor, saw that the marquis was coming out boldly to fight with him, he advanced, he and his people, to meet the marquis. And as they were approaching one another, what does Branas do but put spurs to his horse and put himself ahead of his people a good stone's throw to hasten and fall upon the battle of the marquis. When the marquis saw him coming he spurred forward to meet him, and he struck him full in the eye with the first blow and struck him dead with that blow. Then he struck right and left, he and his people, and they slew many of them. When the others saw that their lord was dead, they began to give way and turned to flee. When the emperor, the traitor, who had had the gates closed on the marquis, saw that they were fleeing, he sallied forth from the city with all his people and began to pursue them. And they gained much booty, the marquis and the others, in the way of horses as well as many other things. Thus did the marquis avenge the emperor on the one who had been besieging him. When they had defeated them, they came back to Constantinople, both the emperor and the marquis, and when they were returned and had laid aside their arms, the emperor thanked the marquis right heartily for avenging him so well on that enemy of his. And then the marquis asked him why he had had the gates closed on him. "Oh, so that is it now!" said the emperor. "Yes, by God!" said the marquis.[53] And it was not long after this that the emperor and his traitors planned a great treason, namely, to have the marquis slain. Finally an old man who learned of it had pity on the marquis and came to him right fairly and said to him: "Lord, for God's sake, go away from this city; for if you are still here the third day from now, the emperor and his traitors have planned a great treason, to take you and have you slain." When the marquis heard this news, he was not at all happy. So he went that very night and had them make ready his galleys, and he put to sea before it

[53] Ba, ensi est ore, fist li empereres; or, de par dieu, fist le marchis.

was day and went away. And he did not stop until he came
to Tyre. Now it happened before this that the land was lost
and the king of Jerusalem [54] was dead and the kingdom of
Jerusalem was all lost and there was not a city which held out,
save only Tyre and Ascalon. Now the king who was dead had
two married sisters. A certain knight, my lord Guy of Lusignan
in Poitou, had to wife the elder, the one to whom the kingdom
had fallen, and my lord Humphrey of Thoron had the
younger.[55] Now one day all the barons of the land and the count
of Tripoli and the Templars and the Hospitallers assembled
in Jerusalem at the Temple and said among themselves that
they would separate my lord Guy from his wife, because the
kingdom had fallen to his wife and they wanted to give her
another husband who was more fitted to be king than my lord
Guy was. And they did so. They separated them, and when
they had separated them, they could never agree on the one
to whom they should marry her, until finally they left it all
to the queen who had been the wife of my lord Guy. So they
gave her the crown and she was to give it to the one whom
she wanted to be king. And so on another day all the barons
and the Templars and the Hospitallers assembled again, and
there was the count of Tripoli, who was the best knight of the
kingdom, and who thought the lady would give him the crown,
and there was my lord Guy, who had had the queen to wife.
When they were all assembled, the lady took the crown and
looked up and down and saw the one who had been her husband,
and she went forward and put it on his head. So my lord Guy was
king.[56] When the count of Tripoli saw this, he was so aggrieved

[54] Baldwin IV died in 1185, shortly before the fall of Jerusalem.

[55] They were half-sisters, daughters of Aymeri I by his first and his
second wife, respectively. The elder was Sibylle, whose first husband was
William Longsword, son of William the Old of Montferrat, and brother
of Conrad and Boniface. The offspring of this marriage was Baldwin V,
who reigned only a year and who is not mentioned by Robert. The younger
was Isabelle, later married to Conrad of Montferrat, as Robert tells.

[56] This romantic tale of the election of Guy of Lusignan is found also in
the Récits d'un ménestrel de Reims (§§ 28 ff.). The editor, De Wailly, implies in the introduction (p. xlv) that this is the earliest appearance of the
story, ignoring Robert's account.

that he went away to his own country, to Tripoli, in wrath.

It was not long afterwards that he [the king] fought with the Saracens and was taken prisoner and all his people were defeated, and the land was lost, so that there was never a city which held out, save only Tyre and Ascalon. When Saladin saw that he had the land in his hands, he came to the king of Jerusalem, whom he had in his prison, and said to him that if he could make them surrender Ascalon to him he would let him go and a large part of his people with him. And the king answered him: "Take me there, then," said he, "and I will make them surrender it to you." And Saladin took him there. When they came there, the king spoke to those of the city and told them to surrender the city, because he willed it so. And they went and surrendered the city to him. When Saladin had the city in his hands, he let the king go and part of his people with him. And the king, when he had thus escaped from prison, went with all the people he had to Tyre. And while the king was doing these things, the marquis had won over all those of Tyre, the Genoese who were there and all the others, to his side, and they had all promised fealty to him and had sworn on relics to hold to him in all things as to their lord, and he would help them defend the city. Now the marquis had found so great dearth in the city that a measure of grain of the city which would not make more than a *sestier* and a half at Amiens, sold for one hundred besants. Now when the king came to Tyre, his sergeants began to call out: "Open, open the gate! Behold the king who comes here." And those within answered that they should not enter, and finally the marquis came to the walls and said that he should not enter. "How now?" said the king. "Am I not lord and king within there?" "By God's name," said the marquis, "you are neither king nor lord, nor shall you enter, for you have brought everything to shame and have lost all the land. And, besides, the dearth is so great within here that, if you and your people should enter, the whole city would be lost through hunger. And I had rather," said the marquis, "that you were lost, you and your people, which would be no

great matter, than we who are within, and the city, too." When
the king saw he could not enter, he turned away with all his
people and went off toward Acre to a certain castle and lodged
there. And he was there until the king of France and the king
of England found him there. Now while the marquis was at
Tyre in that great dearth that was there, God sent them comfort, so that a merchant came bringing a grain ship and offered
at ten besants the grain that had been at a hundred. And the
marquis and all they of the city were right glad of it, and all
the grain was kept and bought in the city.

It was scarcely any time after this that Saladin came and
besieged Tyre both by land and by sea, so that neither food
nor anything else could come into the city, and he sat there so
long that the dearth was again as great in the city as it had
been before.

When the marquis saw that the dearth was so great in the
city and that they could not have relief or comfort from any
quarter, he sent for all those of the city, both the Genoese that
were there and all the others, and he spoke to them and said:
"Lords," said he, "we are in an evil plight, unless God have
mercy on us, for the dearth is so great in the city that there is
scarcely any food or grain by which we can keep ourselves alive
much longer, and no comfort can come either by sea or by land.
'Fore God, if there be any one of you who can offer a plan,
let him do so." And finally a Genoese came forward and said:
"If you are willing to put your trust in me," he said, "I will
give you a good plan." "What then?" said the marquis. "I
will tell you," said he. "We have here in the city certain ships
and galleys and barges and other vessels. Now I will tell you
what I will do. I will take four galleys with me and man them
with the best men we have, and I will put to sea before daybreak, as if I were trying to escape. And as soon as the Saracens
see me, they will not take time to arm themselves, but they will
be in such great haste to come up with me and chase me that
they will not arm themselves at all; instead, they will set sail
after me. And you will have all your other vessels and barges

and galleys right well manned with the best men you have, and when you see that they have all set sail after me and are well under way, then cast loose all your vessels and set sail after them, and I will turn about and we will fight with them. Then God will send us help, if it pleases Him." And they all agreed to this plan and did everything just as he had proposed.

When it came toward day and he had his four galleys right well prepared and right well manned, and all the other vessels also were right well manned, what did he do but put to sea a little before daybreak. Now the sea harbor, by means of which the ships were wont to leave and to enter, was within the walls of the city of Tyre. And he got under way and began to go at a great pace. When he was at a little distance and the Saracens saw him, they made such haste to follow him that they did not arm themselves at all, and they launched all their hundred galleys and began to give chase to him. When they were all well under way, they of the city set sail after them, and those whom the Saracens were chasing turned about. And so the Tyrians came up with these Saracens who were all unarmed, and they slew many of them and defeated them so that of all the hundred galleys only two escaped being taken by the Tyrians. And Saladin was watching all this and lamenting more than a good deal and pulling his beard and tearing his hair for grief at seeing his people cut to pieces before his eyes and he not able to help them. And when he had so lost his navy, he broke camp and went away. So in this way the city was saved by the marquis. And the king Guy was in this small castle near Acre, there where the king of France and the king of England found him later.

It was scarcely any time after this that King Guy was dead and his wife also, and the kingdom fell to the wife of my lord Humphrey of Thoron, she who was sister to the queen. So they went and took his wife away from my lord Humphrey and gave her to the marquis. So the marquis was king, and he had a daughter by her, and then the marquis was slain by the Assassins. Then they took the queen and gave her to Count Henry

of Champagne. And afterwards they besieged Acre and took
it.[57]

Now we have told you the wrong for which the marquis
of Montferrat hated the emperor of Constantinople, and why
he was more at pains and more urgent than all the others that
they should go to Constantinople. So we shall return now to
our earlier matter. After the doge of Venice had said to the
barons that now they had a good excuse for going to the land
of Constantinople and that he was greatly in favor of it, then
all the barons agreed to it. Then the bishops were asked if
it would be a sin to go there, and the bishops answered that
it would not be a sin but rather a righteous deed; for since
they had the rightful heir who had been disinherited, they
could well help him to win his rights and avenge himself on
his enemies. Then they made the youth swear on relics that
he would keep the covenants he had made with them before.

Then all the pilgrims and the Venetians agreed to go there,
and they got ready their fleet and their gear and put to sea.
They went until they came to a port which is called Abydos,[58]
which was a good hundred leagues this side of Constantinople.
Now this was the port where Troy the Great was located, at
the entrance of the Arm of St. George.[59] From there they set
out again and sailed up the Arm of St. George until they came
within a league of Constantinople. Then they waited there
until all the vessels were come together. And when the whole
fleet and all the vessels were come together, they arrayed

[57] In fact, Acre was taken by the crusaders in July, 1191, while Conrad
was assassinated at the end of April, 1192.

[58] *bouke d'ave.* This really means the mouth or strait of Avie (Abydos),
as in Villehardouin's *Boque d'avie;* the letter of Hugh of St. Pol refers
to the city as *portum Bucceaviae.*

[59] *Bras saint jorge.* The Latin form is *Brachium Sancti Georgii.* This name
was applied in the West to the Bosporus at least from the time of the First
Crusade; so the *Gesta Anonymi,* Gilbert of Nogent, Albert of Aix, Odo of
Deuil, William of Tyre, etc. Robert uses it here for the whole extent of
the Straits from the opening of the Hellespont to the end of the Bosporus,
and so does Villehardouin. The name seems to have been derived from
the monastery of St. George of the Mangana, or Arsenal, which stands on
the citadel of Constantinople, overlooking the Bosporus.

and adorned their vessels so finely that it was the most beautiful thing in the world to see. When they of Constantinople
saw this fleet which was so finely arrayed, they gazed at it in
wonder, and they were mounted on the walls and on the
houses to look upon this marvel. And they of the fleet also
regarded the great size of the city, which was so long and so
wide, and they marveled at it exceedingly. Then they passed
by and made port at Chalcedon,[60] across the Arm of St. George.

When the emperor of Constantinople learned of it, he sent
good envoys to ask them what they sought there and why they
were come there, and he sent word to them that if they
wanted any of his gold or his silver, he would right gladly send
it to them. When the high men heard this, they answered the
envoys that they did not want any of his gold or his silver,
but rather they wanted the emperor to surrender the empire,
for he held it neither rightfully nor loyally, and they sent
word to him that they had the rightful heir with them, Alexius,
the son of Isaac the emperor. Thereupon the envoys answered
and said that the emperor would do nothing of the sort, and
with that they went away. Then the doge of Venice spoke to
the barons and said to them: "Lords, I propose that we take
ten galleys and place the youth on one of them and people
with him, and that they go under flag of truce to the shore of
Constantinople and ask those of the city if they would be
willing to recognize the youth as their lord." And the high
men answered that this would be a good thing to do. So they
got ready these ten galleys and the youth and many armed men
with him. And they rowed close to the walls of the city and
rowed up and down, and they showed the youth, whose name
was Alexius, to the people, and they asked them if they recognized him as their lord. And they of the city answered plainly
and said that they did not recognize him as their lord and
did not know who he was. And those who were in the galleys
with the youth said that he was the son of Isaac, the former
emperor, and those within answered again that they did not
know anything about him. Then they came back again to the

[60] *Mauchidone.*

host and made known how the people had answered them. Then it was commanded throughout all the host that all should arm themselves, both great and small. And when they were all armed, they confessed themselves and received communion, for they were very fearful of landing over against Constantinople. Then they ordered their battles and their ships and their transports and their galleys, and the knights entered the transports with their horses, and they got under way. And they had the trumpets sounded, of silver and of brass, fully a hundred pair, and drums and tabors more than a great many.

When the people of the city saw this great navy and this great fleet and heard the sound of the trumpets and the drums, which were making a great din, they all armed themselves and mounted on the houses and on the towers of the city. And it seemed to them very much as if the whole sea and land trembled and as if all the sea were covered with ships. In the meantime, the emperor had made his people come all armed to the shore to defend it.

When the crusaders and the Venetians saw that the Greeks were come to the shore all armed to meet them, they talked together until the doge of Venice said that he would go in advance with all his forces and seize the shore with the help of God. Then he took his ships and his galleys and his transports and put himself in front at the head of the host. Then they took their crossbowmen and their archers and put them in front on barges to clear the shore of the Greeks, and when they were drawn up in this way, they advanced toward the shore. When the Greeks saw that the pilgrims were not going to give up coming to the shore for fear of them, and saw them approaching, they fell back and did not dare wait for them. And so the fleet made the shore. As soon as they had made land, the knights issued forth from the transports on their horses; for the transports were made in such a way that there was a door that could be opened and a bridge thrust out by which the knights could come out on land all mounted. When the fleet had made land and the Greeks who had drawn back saw that they were all come out, they were greatly dismayed at it.

Now these were the same people, these Greeks who had come
to defend the shore, who had boasted to the emperor that the
pilgrims should never land as long as they were there.[61] When
the knights were come forth from the transports, they began to
give chase to these Greeks, and they chased them as far as a
bridge which was near the head of the city.[62] On this bridge there
was a gate through which the Greeks passed in their flight to
Constantinople. When the knights were returned from chasing
these Greeks, they all talked together until the Venetians said
that their vessels would not be in safety unless they were in the
harbor, so they decided to put them in the harbor. Now the harbor of Constantinople [63] was right well secured with a great iron
chain [64] which was fastened at one end in the city and at the
other end, across the harbor, at the tower of Galata. This tower
was very strong and defendable and was right well manned
with defenders.

By the advice of the high men this tower was besieged and
finally taken by force. Now there were Greek galleys placed
along the chain from one end to the other to help defend it.

[61] Villehardouin's account of this landing across from Constantinople (§§
156, 157) deserves to be quoted: "And the morning was fine, a little after
sunrise, and the emperor Alexius was awaiting them with his great battles
and his great forces on the other side. And the trumpets sounded, and each
galley was tied to a transport to cross over more safely. They did not ask
which should go first, but each made for the shore as best it could. And
the knights issued forth from the transports and vaulted into the sea up to
their waists all armed, with helms laced on and swords in hand, and the
good archers and the crossbowmen were each in his place at the landing.
And the Greeks made a show of resisting, but when it came to the lowering
of the lances they turned their backs and yielded them the shore. And
know that never was a port taken more proudly or more worthily. Then
the seamen began to open the doors of the transports and put out the
bridges and lead out the horses, and the knights began to mount the horses
and the battles began to arrange themselves in the order agreed on."
[62] This is the bridge over the stream that flows into the Golden Horn.
Villehardouin says that the Greeks broke it down and the crusaders had to
repair it when they made their march to invest the walls at that corner of
the city.
[63] The Golden Horn; see map facing p. 31.
[64] For this chain, see Van Millingen, Byzantine Constantinople, p. 228. It
is described in the letter of Hugh of St. Pol; Dandulo says that it was
broken by the attack of the great Venetian ship Aquila.

And when the tower was taken and the chain was broken, the vessels entered the harbor and were put in safety, and they captured some of the Greek galleys and ships which were in the harbor. And when the ships and all the other vessels were put within the harbor in safety, all the pilgrims and Venetians assembled and took counsel together as to how they should attack the city. And finally they agreed among them that the French should attack it by land and the Venetians by sea. So the doge of Venice said that he would have engines and ladders made on his ships by which they could assail the walls. Then the knights and all the other pilgrims armed themselves and set out to cross by a bridge which was about two leagues away, and there was no way to cross over to Constantinople less than four leagues from there except at this bridge. And when they came to the bridge, the Greeks came there to dispute the passage with them as best they could, until finally the pilgrims drove them away by force of arms and crossed over. When they came to the city, the high men encamped and pitched their tents in front of the palace of Blachernae, which belonged to the emperor. This palace was right at the head of the city.[65] Then the doge of Venice had marvelous engines made and very fine, for he had them take the spars which carry the sails of the ships,[66] and which were fully thirty *toises*[67] long or more, and he had them well tied and made fast to the masts with strong ropes, and he had them make good bridges of planks on them and good stakes alongside the ropes.[68] And the

---

[65] See map facing p. 31: D.

[66] Venetian and other Italian ships of this time were lateen rigged; that is, the sails were carried by very long spars or yardarms placed diagonally to the masts.

[67] The medieval *toise* was about equivalent to the fathom, or six feet. If Robert is using the term in this sense, his figures are very inaccurate, here as well as elsewhere. Thus his thirty *toises* would make a spar 180 feet long, while the letter of Hugh of St. Pol says they were 100 feet. Later he estimates the two columns of Constantinople as 50 *toises* or 300 feet high, which is about twice the actual height.

[68] *bons puis encoste de cordes.* Jeanroy (*Romania*, LIII, 392-93) suggests *puins* instead of *puis*, and interprets it as hand-grips, ropes stretched on either side of the bridge to serve as hand rails.

bridges were so wide that three knights in armor could go side by side. And the doge had the bridges well protected and covered with hides and canvas on the sides, so that those who mounted to the assault need have no fear of the quarrels of crossbows or of arrows. And the bridges extended so far out beyond the ships that the height from the bridge to the ground was forty *toises* or more. And on each of the transports there was a mangonel which could cast as far as the walls and into the city. When the Venetians had their ships equipped as I have just told you, the pilgrims on the other side, who were attacking by land, had their petraries and their mangonels set up so that they were casting and shooting as far as the palace of the emperor, and those within the city were likewise shooting as far as the tents of the pilgrims. Then they talked together, the pilgrims and the Venetians, and they appointed the morrow for assaulting the city both by land and by sea at the same time. When it was come to the morrow morning and the Venetians were getting ready and ordering their vessels and had drawn as close to the walls as possible for the assault and likewise the pilgrims had their forces drawn up on the other side, behold the emperor of Constantinople, Alexius, sallied forth from the city by a gate called the Roman gate[69] with all his people fully armed and there he arranged his forces and made seventeen battles. In these seventeen battles they counted well nigh a hundred thousand men on horse. Then he sent most of these seventeen battles to surround the camp of the French and the rest he kept with him. And all the men on foot of the city who could bear arms he made to come out and he had them ranged along the walls, between the camp of the French and the walls. When the French saw themselves so surrounded by these battles, they were greatly dismayed. Then they ordered their battles, and they made only seven battles of seven hundred knights, for more they did not have. And of these seven hundred, fifty were on foot.

When they had thus ordered their forces, the count of Flanders asked for the first battle and it was given him, and

[69] The Gate of St. Romanus; see map facing p. 31.

the count of St. Pol and my lord Pierre of Amiens had the second battle, and my lord Henry, brother of the count of Flanders, had the third battle and the Germans. Then they arranged that the sergeants on foot should follow the mounted battles, so that three or four companies followed each mounted battle, and each of the battles had the men of its own country following it. When they had chosen the three battles which were to fight with the emperor, they chose the other four which should guard the camp, so that the marquis, who was lord of the host, had the rear guard and guarded the camp from the rear, and Count Louis had the next one and the Champagners had the third and the Burgundians had the fourth, and the marquis commanded these four battles.[70] Then they took all the horse-boys and cooks who could bear arms and they had them fitted out with quilts and saddle cloths and copper pots and maces and pestles,[71] and they were so ugly and hideous that the common foot soldiers of the emperor, who were in front of the walls, had great fear and terror when they saw them. The four battles which I have just now named you guarded the camp, for fear that the battles of the emperor which surrounded it should break through and harm the camp and the tents. And they placed the horse-boys and the cooks on the side toward the city, opposite the emperor's foot soldiers, who were ranged along the walls. When the emperor's foot soldiers saw our common people so hideously arrayed, they had so great fear and so great terror of them that they never dared move or come toward them, so the camp was not in danger from that side.

Then it was ordered that the count of Flanders and the

[70] This arrangement of battles and commanders agrees almost exactly with that given by Villehardouin (§§ 147 ff.): (1) Baldwin of Flanders; (2) Henry, his brother, with Matthew of Warlincourt and Baldwin of Beauvoir; (3) Hugh of St. Pol with Pierre of Amiens; (4) Louis of Blois; (5) Matthew of Montmorency and the Champagners; (6) the Burgundians; and (7) Boniface of Montferrat with the Lombards, Tuscans, and Germans.

[71] *de keutes pointes et de peniax et de pos de cuivre et de piletes et de pestiax*; *piletes* and *pestiax* mean about the same, instruments used for braying material in mortars.

count of St. Pol and my lord Henry, who had the three
battles, should fight with the emperor. And the other four
battles were forbidden to move from their place, no matter
what need the others might have—unless they should see that
they were about to be destroyed—for fear that they should be
cut off and attacked by the battles which were around the
camp. In the meantime, while the French were drawn up for
battle in this way, the Venetians, who were on the sea, did not
neglect their part, but they worked their ships close to the
walls, so that they mounted right onto the walls of the city
by the ladders and bridges which they had made on the ships.
And they shot and hurled and cast missiles with their mangonels and assaulted more fiercely than a great deal, until
finally they set fire to the city so that there was burned of it
a part fully as large as the city of Arras.[72] But they did not dare
deploy or advance into the city, for they were too few and
could not have held out. So they withdrew again to their ships.

On the other side, the high men who were to fight with the
emperor had arranged that two of the worthiest and wisest
men should be chosen in each battle, and whatever they commanded, it was to be done. If they commanded "Spur!" they
should spur, and if they commanded "Trot!" they should trot.
The count of Flanders, who had the van, rode ahead at a trot
against the emperor. And the emperor was fully a quarter of
a league distant from the count of Flanders, and he made his
battles ride forward to meet the count. The count of St. Pol
and my lord Pierre of Amiens, who had the next battle, rode
a little behind at one side, and my lord Henry of Hainault and
the Germans, who had the third battle, rode next. And there
was no horse that was not covered with coat of arms or cloth
of silk over all the other coverings. And three companies, or
four or five, of sergeants on foot followed each of the battles

[72] According to Nicetas (pp. 722 ff.) this, the first of three disastrous
fires, consumed everything in the section extending from the region of
the palace of Blachernae to the monastery of Christ the Benefactor, which
stands to the east near the Golden Horn, perhaps a third of the length of
that side of the triangle. See also Villehardouin, § 176.

at the tails of the horses. And they rode so well in line and so close together that no man of them was so bold as to dare ride ahead of the others. And the emperor rode forward to meet our people with all of nine battles, and there was no one of these nine battles in which there were not three thousand knights, or four or five there were in some of them. Now when the count of Flanders had advanced from the camp two full bowshots, his advisers said to him: "Lord, you do not well to go to fight the emperor so far away from the camp, for if you fight him there and have need of help, those who are guarding the camp will not be able to help you. If you take our advice, you will return to the lists,[73] and there you will await the emperor more safely, if he wants to fight." So the count of Flanders turned back to the lists, as he was advised, and the battle of my lord Henry also. And the count of St. Pol and my lord Pierre of Amiens did not want to turn back, but they came to a halt in the midst of the field with all their forces. When the battle of the count of St. Pol and my lord Pierre of Amiens saw the count of Flanders turn back, they all said to one another that the count of Flanders did great shame to turn back, he who had been given the van. And they all said: "Lords, lords, the count of Flanders is turning back. Now that he draws back, he leaves you the van, so let us take it, in God's name!" So the barons agreed together and said they would take the van. Now when the count of Flanders saw that the count of St. Pol and my lord Pierre of Amiens would not turn back, he sent word to them by a messenger and besought them to retire. And my lord Pierre of Amiens sent back word that they would not do so. Then the count of Flanders sent word to him again by two messengers, begging him for God's sake not to do them this shame but to turn back as they themselves had been advised to do. And the count of St. Pol and my lord Pierre of Amiens sent back word again, nay, nay, they would not turn back. Then came my lord Pierre of Amiens and my lord Eustace of Canteleux, who were the

---

[73] *lisches*, palisades that had been erected around the camp, as Villehardouin tells (§ 166), and also the letter of Hugh of St. Pol.

captains of that battle, and they said: "Lords, ride forward now, in God's name, all at the trot." And they began to advance at the trot. And all those of the host who had remained behind began to cry out after them: "See, see! The count of St. Pol and my lord Pierre of Amiens mean to attack the emperor! Lord God," they began to say and to cry, "Lord God, guard them this day and all their company. See! They have taken the van that belonged to the count of Flanders. Lord God, bring them to safety!" And the ladies and maidens of the palace were mounted to the windows, and the other people of the city, both ladies and maidens, were mounted on the walls of the city, and were watching this battle ride forward and the emperor on the other side. And they were saying to one another that our men seemed like angels, they were so beautiful, because they were so finely armed and their horses so finely accoutered.

When the knights of the battle of the count of Flanders saw that the count of St. Pol and my lord Pierre of Amiens would not turn back for anything, they came to the count and said to him: "Lord, you are doing great shame not to advance, and know that if you do not now ride forward, we will no longer hold ourselves bound to you." [74] When the count of Flanders heard this, he put spurs to his horse, and all the others after him, and they spurred forward until they came up with the battle of the count of St. Pol and my lord Pierre of Amiens, and when they had come up with them, they rode beside them all on one front, and the battle of my lord Henry rode after them. The battles of the emperor and our battles were now so close together that the emperor's crossbowmen were shooting into the midst of our people and our crossbowmen likewise into the midst of the emperor's people. Now there was only a small rise of ground to mount between the emperor and our battles, and the battles of the emperor began to mount on one side and ours on the other. When our people came to the top of the rise and the emperor saw them, he halted and

[74] The manuscript reads: *nous ne vous tenrons plus a nous.* It undoubtedly should read, as Jeanroy (*loc. cit.*) suggests: *nous ne nous tenrons plus a vous.*

all his people also, and they were so startled and dismayed to
see our battles riding thus front to front against them, that
they did not know what to do. And while they were standing
there so confused, the other battles of the emperor, which had
been sent to surround the camp of the French, drew off and
joined the emperor all together in the valley. When the French
saw all the battles of the emperor assembled together, they
came to a halt on the top of the rise, wondering what the
emperor would do. And the counts and high men of the three
battles sent messengers to one another to take counsel as to
what they should do, whether they should advance against the
army of the emperor or not. And they decided not to go on,
for they were very far from the camp, and if they should fight
there where the emperor was, those who were guarding the
camp would not see them nor be able to help them, if there
should be need of it. And, besides, between them and the
emperor there was a great canal, a great conduit, by which
the water came into Constantinople, and if they should cross
over it, they would suffer great loss of their forces. So, because of this, they decided not to go on. While the French
were thus talking together, behold the emperor drew back into
Constantinople. And when he was come there he was right
harshly blamed by the ladies and maidens, and by one and all,
because he had not fought against so few people as the French
were, with so great a force as he had had with him.

When the emperor had retreated in this way, the pilgrims
went back to their tents and disarmed, and when they were disarmed, the Venetians, who had crossed over in ships and barges,
came to ask news of them. And they said: "I'faith, we heard
that you were fighting with the Greeks, and we were greatly
afraid for you, so we came over to help you." And the French
answered them and said: "I'faith, we have done right well,
God be thanked, for we went out against the emperor and the
emperor did not dare join battle with us." Then the French in
turn asked the Venetians for their news, and they said:
"I'faith," said they, "we attacked right fiercely, and we entered

into the city over the walls, and we set fire in the city so that a large part of it was burned."

While the French and the Venetians were talking together, there arose a great clamor in the city, for they of the city told the emperor that he ought to deliver them from the French who were besieging them, and that if he did not fight with them they would seek out the youth whom the French had brought and make him emperor and lord over them.

When the emperor heard this, he gave them his word that he would fight them on the morrow. But when it came near midnight, the emperor fled from the city with as many people as he could take with him.

When the morning was come on the morrow and they of the city knew that the emperor was fled, what do they do but go to the gates and open them and issue forth and come to the camp of the French and ask and inquire for Alexius, the son of Isaac. And they were told that they would find him at the tent of the marquis. When they came there, they found him, and his friends did him great honor and made great rejoicing over him. And they thanked the barons right heartily and said that they who had done this thing had done right well and had done a great deed of baronage. And they said that the emperor had fled, and that they [the crusaders] should come into the city and into the palace as if it all belonged to them. Then all the high barons of the host assembled, and they took Alexius, the son of Isaac, and they led him to the palace with great joy and much rejoicing. And when they were come to the palace, they had Isaac, his father, brought out of prison, and his wife also. This was the one who had been imprisoned by his brother, the recent emperor. When Isaac was out of prison, he made great rejoicing over his son and embraced and kissed him, and he gave great thanks to the barons who were there and said that it was by the help of God first and next by theirs that he was out of prison. Then they brought two golden chairs and seated Isaac on one and Alexius his son on the other beside him, and to Isaac was given the imperial seat. Then they said to the emperor: "Sire, there is a high man here in prison, Murzuphlus[75] is his name, who has been there full seven years. If it be your will, it would be a good thing to set him free." So this Murzuphlus was brought out of prison, and the emperor made him his chief steward, for which the emperor afterwards had most evil reward, as we shall tell you later. Now it happened, after the French had done these things, that the sultan of Konia[76] heard how the French had done these things. So he came to talk with them there where they were still quartered outside of Constantinople, and he said to them: "Surely, lords," said he, "you have done a very great deed of baronage and of prowess to have conquered so mighty a place as Constantinople, which is the head of the world, and to have put the rightful heir of Constantinople on his throne and crowned him emperor." For they say in that country that Constantinople is the head of the world. "Lords," said the sultan, "there is something I want to ask you for. I have a brother younger than myself who has taken from me by treason my land and seigniory of Konia, of which I was lord and of which I am the rightful heir. If you will help me recover my land and seigniory, I will give you right plentifully of my wealth, and will have myself baptized a Christian and all those who hold of me, if I can have again my seigniory with your help." And the barons answered that they would take counsel on it. So word was sent to the doge of Venice and to

[75] *Morchofles;* Alexius Ducas, nicknamed Murzuphlus, according to Nicetas, on account of the heavy eyebrows which grew together over the bridge of his nose. This name appears in various forms in Western chronicles: Villehardouin has Morchuflex; Gunther, Murtiphlo (which he translates *flos cordis,* "flower of the heart"!); the letter of Emperor Baldwin, Marculphus, etc. He belonged to a leading family in Constantinople which had furnished two emperors: Constantine X, 1059-67, and Michael VII, 1071-78. Gunther, whose authority in such matters is not great, says that he was the ringleader in the earlier conspiracy to dethrone Isaac and put his brother Alexius on the throne.

[76] Caichosroes; he was driven from the country by his brother, Rokn-Eddin (Nicetas, p. 688; Muralt, *Essai de chronographie byzantine,* p. 260). He had sought and secured help from Emperor Manuel, but was defeated and found refuge in the Greek empire. Nicetas speaks of him again in 1205 as having recently recovered his kingdom.

the marquis and all the high barons, and they assembled in a great council, and finally it was their decision that they would not do what the sultan asked of them. And when they came from their council they answered the sultan that they could not do what he asked of them, because they had still to get their reward from the emperor, and it would be dangerous to leave Constantinople, as things were then, and they dared not leave it. When the sultan heard this, he was very angry and went away again.

Then when the barons had taken Alexius to the palace, they asked about the sister of the king of France who was called the French empress, if she were still living. And they said yes, and that she was married; that a high man of the city, Branas was his name, had married her, and she was living in a palace near there. So the barons went there to see her, and they saluted her and made her many fair offers of service, but she met them with very bad grace and was very angry with them, because they had come there and had had this Alexius crowned. And she was unwilling to talk with them but had an interpreter talk for her, and the interpreter said that she did not know any French at all. But Count Louis, who was her cousin,[77] made himself known to her.

Afterwards it happened that the barons went one day for diversion to the palace to see Isaac and the emperor his son. And while the barons were there at the palace, a king came there whose skin was all black, and he had a cross in the middle of his forehead that had been made with a hot iron. This king was living in a very rich abbey in the city, in which the former emperor Alexius had commanded that he should be lodged and of which he was to be lord and owner as long as he wanted to stay there. When the emperor saw him coming, he rose to meet him and did great honor to him. And the emperor asked the barons: "Do you know," said he, "who this man is?" "Not at all, sire," said the barons. "I'faith," said the emperor, "this is the king of Nubia, who is come on

[77] In fact, she was the aunt of Louis, count of Blois, whose mother Alix was her half-sister.

pilgrimage to this city." Then they had an interpreter talk to
him and ask him where his land was, and he answered the
interpreter in his own language that his land was a hundred
days' journey still beyond Jerusalem, and he had come from
there to Jerusalem on pilgrimage. And he said that when he
set out from his land he had fully sixty of his countrymen with
him, and when he came to Jerusalem there were only ten of
them alive, and when he came from Jerusalem to Constantinople there were only two of them alive. And he said that he
wanted to go on pilgrimage to Rome and from Rome to St.
James,[78] and then come back to Jerusalem, if he should live
so long, and then die there. And he said that all the people
of his land were Christians and that when a child was born and
baptized they made a cross in the middle of his forehead with
a hot iron, like the one he had. And the barons gazed at this
king with great wonder.[79]

Then when the barons had crowned Alexius, as I have told
you, it was arranged that my lord Pierre of Bracheux, he and
his people, should stay in the palace with the emperor. And
then afterwards the barons arranged how they should be
lodged, and they did not dare remain in the city at all, because
of the Greeks who were traitors, but instead they went to take
quarters across the harbor, over toward the tower of Galata.
And they found lodging there all together in certain houses
that were there and they drew their navy up to the shore in
front of them. And they went to the city whenever they
wanted to, and when they wanted to go by water they crossed
over on barges, and when they wanted to go on horseback they

[78] Santiago of Compostela, in the northwestern corner of Spain, where the
body of St. James the Greater, the evangelist of Spain, was said to be preserved, having been brought there miraculously after his martyrdom in
Judea.

[79] This reads like a real incident, heard by Robert at near hand. According
to Jacques de Vitry, who learned about them while in the East on the Fifth
Crusade, the Nubians were Jacobite Christians, that is, followers of the
Monophysite heresy which attributed only one nature to Christ; they burn
their children on the forehead with a hot iron in the form of a cross before
they baptize them.

passed over by the bridge. Then when they had taken quarters, the French and the Venetians agreed between them to have fifty *toises* of the walls of the city torn down, for they feared that those of the city might turn against them.

Then all the high barons assembled one day at the palace of the emperor and demanded their bargain of the emperor. And he answered that he would surely keep it, but that he wished first to be crowned.[80] So they chose and fixed a day for crowning him. And on that day he was crowned in high state as emperor with the consent of his father, who granted it right willingly. And when he was crowned, the barons demanded their payment again, and he said he would gladly pay them as much as he could, and he paid them then a good hundred thousand marks. Of these hundred thousand marks the Venetians received a half, for they were to have half of the gains, and of the fifty thousand marks that remained they were paid the thirty-six thousand which the French still owed them for their navy. And from the other twenty thousand [*sic*] marks which remained to the pilgrims they paid back those who had loaned their money to pay for the passage.

Afterwards the emperor sought out the barons and said to them that he had nothing save Constantinople and that this was worth little to him by itself, for his uncle held all the cities and castles that ought to be his. So he asked the barons to help him conquer some of the land around, and he would right gladly give them still more of his wealth. Then they answered that they would be very glad to do it, and that anyone who wanted to profit by this could go. Then a good half of the host went with Alexius and the other half stayed in Constantinople to receive the payment, and Isaac stayed behind to make the payment to the barons. So Alexius went with all his host and conquered full twenty cities and full forty castles or more of the land, and Alexius, the other emperor, his uncle, fled always before him, and the French were away fully three months with

[80] In the preceding paragraph Robert speaks of Alexius as already crowned, but this refers apparently to his having been recognized as emperor along with his father, and not to any actual coronation.

Alexius. In the meantime, while Alexius was making this raid,
they of Constantinople had their wall rebuilt stronger and
higher than it had been before, for the French had had fully
fifty *toises* of it torn down when they had taken the city, because
they feared the Greeks might turn against them.[81] When the
barons who had remained behind to receive the payment saw
that Isaac was not paying them anything, they sent word to
the other barons who had gone with Alexius to come back,
because Isaac was not making the payments, and to be back before the Feast of All Saints. When the barons heard this, they
told the emperor that they were going back, and when the
emperor heard this he said that he would go back too, since they
were returning, for he dared not trust himself to his Greeks.
So they came back to Constantinople, and the emperor went
to his palace and the pilgrims went to their quarters across
the harbor.

Then the counts and the high men and the doge and the
emperor assembled together. And the French demanded their
payment of the emperor and the emperor answered that he had
spent so much in recovering his city and people that he had
nothing left to pay them with, but if they would give him a
little time he would make arrangements so as to be able to pay
them. So they gave him this respite and when the time was
past, still he did not pay them anything, and the barons demanded their payment again. And again the emperor asked for
a respite and they gave it to him. In the meantime his followers
and people and this Murzuphlus whom he had freed from
prison came to him and said: "Ah, sire, you have already paid

[81] Alexius was crowned on August 1, 1203, and set out shortly after from
Constantinople to drive his uncle, Alexius III, out of the land. On August
19 another disastrous fire broke out. According to Nicetas (pp. 731 ff.), this
was started by a gang of Flemings and Latins of Constantinople who had
got into a street fight with the populace. He says that it swept across the
narrow part of the city from the Golden Horn to the Sea of Marmora,
endangering Saint Sophia itself, injuring the side of the Hippodrome, and
wiping out the porticoes of the Royal Street and a large portion of the
richest part of the city. Villehardouin (§§ 203 ff.) also gives a vivid description of this conflagration, which was witnessed with grief and pity
by the crusaders from their quarters across the Golden Horn.

them too much! Do not pay them any more. You have
paid them so much now that you have mortgaged everything.
Make them go away and dismiss them from your land." And
Alexius hearkened to this counsel and became unwilling to
pay them anything. When this respite was past and the French
saw that the emperor was not going to pay them anything, all
the counts and the high men of the host came together, and
they went to the palace of the emperor and asked again for their
payment. Then the emperor answered them that he could not
pay them anything, and the barons answered that if he did
not pay them they would seize enough of his possessions to pay
themselves.

With these words the barons departed from the palace and
returned to their quarters, and when they were returned they
took counsel together as to what they should do. And finally
they sent two knights to the emperor and summoned him again
to send them their payment.[82] And he replied to the envoys
that he would not pay them anything and that he had already
paid them too much and that he was not a bit afraid of them;
instead he sent word to them to go away and vacate his land,
and let them know well that if they did not do so shortly he
would do them harm. Thereupon the envoys came back and
made known to the barons what the emperor had replied. And
the barons, when they heard this, considered what they should
do, until finally the doge of Venice said that he would go and
talk to him. So he sent word to him by a messenger to come
and talk with him at the harbor. And the emperor came there
on horseback, and the doge had them man four galleys and he
entered one and had the three others go along to guard him.
And when he came to the shore of the harbor, he saw the
emperor, who had come there on horseback, and he spoke to
him and said: "Alexius, what dost thou mean?" said the doge.
"Take thought how we rescued thee from great wretchedness

---

[82] Villehardouin (§ 211) says that the embassy chosen by the host to carry
the message of defiance to Isaac and Alexius was composed of Conon of
Béthune, Miles of Brabant, and himself for the crusaders, and three others
for the doge.

and how we have made thee a lord and have had thee crowned emperor. Wilt thou not," said the doge, "keep thy covenant with us and wilt thou not do anything more about it?" "Nay," said the emperor, "I will not do any more than I have done." "No?" said the doge. "Wretched boy, we dragged thee out of the filth," said the doge, "and into the filth we will cast thee again. And I defy thee, and I give thee well to know that I will do thee all the harm in my power from this moment forward."

With these words the doge left and went back. And the counts and all the high men of the host and the Venetians assembled together to take counsel as to what they should do. And the Venetians said that they could not set up their ladders and engines on the ships because of the weather which was too cold, for the season was between the Feast of All Saints and Christmas. While they were there in such straits, what did the emperor and his traitors who were with him do but plan a great treason: they wanted . . .[83] take ships into the city by night and have them filled with wood that was well dried and with pieces of fat along with the wood and have them set on fire. When it came toward midnight and the ships were well ablaze, a strong wind arose and the Greeks loosed these ships all on fire to burn the navy of the French, and the wind drove them at a great rate toward the navy. When the Venetians saw this they hastily mounted their barges and galleys and did so well that by God's mercy the navy had no harm. And it was not more than a fortnight after that the Greeks did the same thing again, and when the Venetians saw them again, they went out again to meet them and they defended their navy right well from this fire, so that, by God's mercy, they had no harm from it, save for one merchant ship which had come there. This was burned. Now the dearth was so great in the camp, that a *sestier* of wine was sold there for twelve sous, fourteen sous, even at times fifteen sous, and a hen for twenty sous and an egg for two pennies. But there was no such scarcity of biscuit; rather they had enough to supply the host for some time.

[83] Here the manuscript is blank for the space of four lines.

In the meantime, while they were staying there that winter, they of the city strengthened their defenses right well, and they had their walls and towers raised higher, and they had strong wooden towers built on top of the stone towers, and they had these wooden towers well fitted with projecting hoardings made of sound timbers and well covered with good hides, so that they need not fear the ladders of the Venetian ships. The walls were a good sixty feet high and the towers a hundred. Then they had full forty petraries ranged along the walls within the city, there where it was thought the assault would take place. And it is no wonder that they did all this, for they had plenty of leisure for it. While these things were going on, those of the Greeks who were traitors toward the emperor and this Murzuphlus whom the emperor had freed from prison came together and plotted a great treason. For they wanted to make someone else emperor, someone who would deliver them from the French, because Alexius did not seem good to them any longer. And finally Murzuphlus said: "If you will leave it to me," said he, "and will make me emperor, I will deliver you from the French and from this emperor, so that you will never have any more trouble from them." And they said that if he would deliver them they would make him emperor, and Murzuphlus vowed to free them within a week, and they agreed to make him emperor.

Then Murzuphlus went and lost no time. He took sergeants with him and entered by night into the chamber where his lord the emperor, who had freed him from prison, was sleeping, and he had them tie a cord around his neck and strangle him and his father Isaac also.[84] When he had done this, he went to those who were going to make him emperor and told them of it, and they went and crowned him emperor. When Murzuphlus was emperor, the cry went about through the city: "What is this? I'faith, Murzuphlus is emperor! He has murdered his lord." Then a letter was shot from the city into the camp of

[84] According to Nicetas (p. 744), Isaac had already died, worn out with his many troubles. Villehardouin (§ 223) also says that Isaac died before the murder of Alexius.

the pilgrims to tell them that Murzuphlus had done this thing. When the barons knew about it, some said: "A curse on anyone who cares whether Alexius is dead or not"—because he had not wanted to keep his covenant with the pilgrims. Others said that it weighed on them that he had met his death in this way. It was not long afterwards that Murzuphlus sent word to the count of Flanders, to Count Louis, to the marquis, and to all the other high barons, telling them to go away and vacate his land, and letting them know that he was emperor and that if he came on them there a week from then he would slay them all. When the barons heard the message that Murzuphlus had sent, they replied: "What?" said they, "He who has treacherously murdered his lord by night has sent this word to us?" And they sent back word to him that they defied him and let him now beware of them, for they would not abandon the siege until they had avenged him whom he had murdered and had taken Constantinople again and had secured in full the payment which Alexius had promised them.

When Murzuphlus heard this, he commanded the walls and towers to be well manned and fitted with hoardings, so that they need not fear the attack of the French. And they did this right well, so that the walls and towers were stronger and more defendable than before.

Now it happened—in that time when Murzuphlus the traitor was emperor, and when the host of the French was so impoverished as I have told you, and when they were hardily preparing their ships and their engines for the assault—that John the Vlach [85] sent word to the high barons that if they would crown him king so that he would be lord of his land of Vlachia, he would hold his land and kingdom from them and would come to their aid to help them take Constantinople with all of a

[85] The famous Joannissa, king of the Vlachs and Bulgarians. He called himself Calojohannes ("John the Fair" or "the Good") and is addressed by this title in the letters of Innocent III. Robert was misinformed about his origin. He was the youngest of three brothers who were either Bulgarians or Vlachs, and he had succeeded to the rule of these peoples when his two brothers were assassinated in 1196. It was his older brother, Assen, whom a Greek attendant struck with a whip (Nicetas, p. 482).

hundred thousand men. Now Vlachia is a land which belongs to the emperor, and this John was once a sergeant of the emperor, having charge of one of the emperor's horse farms, so that when the emperor sent for sixty horses or a hundred, this John would send them to him. And he used to come to court every year, before he came into ill favor at the court. And he went there one day, and a eunuch, one of the attendants of the emperor, did him a villainous deed; he struck him across the face with a whip, from which he had great dole. And for this evil deed that was done to him, John the Vlach left the court in wrath and went away to Vlachia. Now Vlachia is a very strong land which is all inclosed by mountains so that one can neither enter nor leave it save by a narrow pass.

When John the Vlach was come there, he began to win over the high men of Vlachia, like one who was a rich man and had some power, and he began to promise and to give to one and to another, and he wrought so that all those of the country were soon subject to him and he was lord over them. When he was lord over them, he went to the Comans[86] and he wrought so with one and another that he became their friend and they were all in his service and he was just like their lord. Now Comania is a land bordering on Vlachia, and I will tell you what kind of people the Comans are. They are a savage people, who neither plow nor sow, and they have neither huts nor houses, but they have tents made of felt in which they shelter themselves, and they live on milk and cheese and flesh. In the summer there are so many flies and gnats that they scarcely dare come out of their tents at all before winter. In winter they come out of their tents and sally forth from their country when they want to make a raid. Now we will tell you what they do. Each one has at least ten or twelve horses, and they have them so well trained that they follow them wherever they want to take them, and they mount first on one and then on another. When they are on a raid, each horse has a bag hung on his

[86] The Comans or Cumans were a tribe of Turkish origin, occupying at this time a large territory north of the Danube. They were in fact allies of Joannissa, who is said to have married a Coman wife.

nose in which his fodder is put, and he feeds as he follows his master, and they do not stop going by night or by day. And they ride so hard that they cover in one day and one night fully six days' journey, or seven or eight. And while they are on the way they will not seize anything or carry it along, before their return, but when they are returning, then they seize plunder and make captives and take anything they can get. Nor do they go armed, except that they wear a garment of sheepskin and carry bows and arrows. They do not worship anything except the first animal encountered in the morning, and the one who encounters it worships it all that day, whatever animal it may be. Now John the Vlach had these Comans in his service and he used to come every year to raid the emperor's lands, even up to Constantinople, and the emperor was not strong enough to defend himself against him. When the barons heard what John the Vlach was asking of them, they said they would consider it, and when they had taken counsel, they came to a bad decision; for they answered that they cared nothing for him nor for his help, but he should know well that they would hurt him and do him harm if they could. And he paid them very dearly for this later. This was a very great mischance and a very great misfortune. Now when he had failed with them, he sent to Rome for his crown, and the apostolic sent a cardinal to crown him, and so he was crowned king.[87]

Now we will tell you of another adventure, one that befell my lord Henry, brother of the count of Flanders. In the midst of these events, while the French were besieging Constantinople, it happened that my lord Henry and those of his company found themselves not at all well off, but rather in great need of food as well as of other things. Finally they heard of a city, Philea was its name, which was ten leagues distant from the camp. This city was very rich and plenteous. So what did

[87] Innocent III had been trying for some time to bring the Bulgarian church into the Latin communion. Papal letters dated February 25, 1204 (Potthast, *Regesta*, I, nos. 2135 ff.), announce the sending of Cardinal Leo with a diadem and scepter, and with the authority to crown Joannissa and to confer the dignity of primate on Basil, archbiship of Trnovo.

my lord Henry do but get ready his gear and set out from the camp by night for this place with thirty knights and many mounted sergeants, in such a way that scarcely anyone knew of it. When he came to the city he did his deed and stayed there a day. Now while he was going there he was spied on, and it was reported to Murzuphlus. When Murzuphlus heard of it, he got together a good thousand mounted men at arms, and he took with him the icon,[88] an image of Our Lady which the Greeks call by this name and which the emperors carry with them when they go to battle. They have so great faith in this icon that they fully believe that no one who carries it in battle can be defeated, and we believe that it was because Murzuphlus had no right to carry it that he was defeated. Now the French had already sent their booty to the camp, and Murzuphlus laid a trap for them on the return. When he came within a league of our men, he put his men in hiding and made his ambush, and our people knew nothing of it. So they were coming back hardily, knowing nothing about this trap. When the Greeks saw them, they cried out and our French looked about them. When they saw them, they had great fear and began to call much upon God and Our Lady and were so dismayed that they did not know what to do. Finally they said to one another: "I'faith! if we flee we are all dead men. It becomes us better to die fighting than fleeing." Then they came to a halt and they brought up eight crossbowmen whom they had with them and put them in front. And the emperor Murzuphlus the traitor and the Greeks came at them at a great pace and fell upon them right fiercely, but never, by God's mercy, did they unhorse a one of the French. When the French saw the Greeks rushing upon them thus from all sides, they let fall their lances and drew the knives and daggers which they had with them and began to defend themselves right hardily, and they slew many of them. When the Greeks saw that the French were having the better of them, they began to lose heart and turned to flee. But our French caught up with them and slew many of them and captured many and took much booty. And they pursued the

[88] *ansconne.*

emperor Murzuphlus a good half league, because they kept
thinking they would catch him. They were in such haste, he
and those of his company, that they let fall the icon and his
imperial helmet and the standard and the icon [*sic*], which was
all of gold and charged with precious stones and was so beautiful and so rich that never was one seen to equal it. When the
French saw this, they left off their pursuit, and they were ex-
ceeding glad and they took the image and brought it along
with great joy and rejoicing. In the meantime, while the fight
was going on, the news came to the camp that they had encountered the Greeks, and when they of the camp heard this
news they armed themselves and spurred forth to meet Lord
Henry and bring him help. But when they came there the
Greeks were already fled and our French were bringing back
the booty, and they were carrying along the icon, which was
as rich and beautiful as I have told you. When they came near
the camp, the bishops and the clerks who were in the camp came
out in procession to meet them and they received the icon with
great joy and rejoicing, and it was entrusted to the bishop of
Troyes. So the bishop carried it into the camp, to a church to
which they all repaired, and the bishops chanted a service, and
they made great rejoicing over it. And from the very day on
which it was captured, the barons all decreed that it should be
given to Cîteaux, and later it was taken there.[89] Now when

---

[89] This incident of the raid of Count Henry and the capture of the icon
seems to have made a great impression at the time. It is reported in Villehardouin, in the *Devastatio*, in the letter of Emperor Baldwin, and in the
general chronicles of Robert of Auxerre, Alberic of Trois-Fontaines, and
others. Alberic (*Recueil des historiens des Gaules et de la France*, XVIII,
768) gives a detailed account which is apparently based on some first-hand
source; the editor, Dom Brial, suggested the lost chronicle of Bishop Nivelon
of Soissons, once seen by Du Cange, but the rediscovery of this manuscript
(published in Riant, *Exuviae*, I, 1-9) has shown that this is wrong. As Riant
says (*Dépouilles*, p. 36), it seems impossible to identify the particular icon.
Some authorities describe it as the portrait of the Blessed Virgin painted by
St. Luke, which was kept in the church of the Virgin called the Hodogetria
and which was the palladium of Constantinople, but it is almost certainly
not this. A charter of Baldwin II, 1247, conferring certain relics upon the
Sainte Chapelle of Paris (Riant, *Exuviae*, II, 134 f.), mentions a triumphal
cross which the emperors used to carry as a talisman of victory. The attribu-

Murzuphlus came back to Constantinople, he made them believe that he had overcome and defeated Lord Henry and his people, and some of the Greeks asked him outright, "Where is the icon and the standard?" And the others said that everything had been put away in safekeeping. This news went up and down until the French heard that Murzuphlus had really made them believe that he had defeated the French. So what do the French do but have a galley manned and the icon taken and raised high up on this galley, and the imperial standard along with it, and they made this galley, all with the icon and the standard, go up and down in front of the walls, so that those who were on the walls and many people of the city saw it and knew well that it was the standard and the icon of the emperor.

When the Greeks saw this, they came to Murzuphlus and began to deride him and reproach him for losing the imperial standard and the icon and for making them believe he had defeated the French. And when Murzuphlus heard this, he excused himself the best he could and began to say: "Now be not dismayed, for I will make them pay dearly for this, and I will avenge myself well on them."

Afterwards it came about that all the French and all the Venetians assembled to take counsel together as to how they should set to work and what they should do and whom they should make emperor, if they should take the city. And finally they decided among them to take ten French of the most worthy men of the host, and ten Venetians likewise of the most worthy men known among them, and whatever these twenty should decide, that should be held to; and in this way, that if the emperor should be chosen from the French, the patriarch should be chosen from the Venetians. And it was decided that the one who should be emperor should have the fourth part of the empire and the fourth part of the city for his own, and the other three parts should be divided so that the Venetians should have one half and the pilgrims the other, and every-

tion to Cîteaux is referred to in most of the sources, but apparently it never reached there.

thing should be held from the emperor.[90] When they had arranged all this, then all they of the host were made to swear on relics that they would bring straight to the camp all the spoils of gold and silver and new cloth to the value of five sous or more, save tools and food, and that they would not use force with any woman or despoil her of any garment she was wearing, for whoever should be found guilty of this would be slain. And they were made to swear on relics that they would not lay hands on monk or on clerk or on priest, unless it be in self-defense, nor break into church or monastery.

Afterwards, when all this was done, Christmas was past and it was near the beginning of Lent, and the Venetians and the French again got themselves ready and prepared their ships. And the Venetians again had bridges made on their ships, and the French had other engines made, which are called "cats" and "carts" and "sows,"[91] to mine the walls. And the Venetians took house timbers and covered their ships with them, joining the boards together, and then they took grapevines and covered the boards with them, so that the petraries might not crush the ships or break them to pieces. And the Greeks strengthened their city mightily within, and they had the wooden towers which were on top of the stone towers well covered with good hides on the outside, and there was no wooden tower that did not have seven stories, or six or five at least.

Then it came about on a Friday, about ten days before Palm Sunday,[92] that the pilgrims and the Venetians got their ships and their engines ready and prepared for the assault. So they ranged their ships side by side, and the French had their engines loaded on barges and galleys, and they set out to go toward the

---

[90] The texts of the treaties between the crusaders and the Venetians (in March, 1204) are published in Tafel and Thomas, I, 444 ff. Dandulo (Muratori, XII, col. 324 ff.) also gives the substance of the agreement.

[91] *cas et carchloies et truis:* the usual Old French descriptive names for wooden housings on wheels, under cover of which the besiegers could approach the walls. See Enlart, *Manuel*, II, 434.

[92] *pasques flouries;* in 1204 Palm Sunday fell on April 18, so the "Friday about ten days before" would be April 9. Villehardouin (§ 236) also gives Friday, April 9, as the day of this attack.

city, and the navy extended fully a good league along its front. And all the pilgrims and the Venetians were right well armed. Now there was a mound within the city, in that quarter where the assault was to be made, which could be plainly seen from the ships over the wall, so high it was. And Murzuphlus the traitor, the emperor, was come to this mound with some of his people, and he had his vermilion tents set up there, and he had his silver trumpets sounded and his timbrels and made a great din, and it was so that the pilgrims could see him plainly and he could see plainly onto the ships of the pilgrims.

When the navy was about to make land, they took strong cables and drew their ships as close as they could to the walls, and the French had their engines set up, their "cats" and "carts" and "sows," to mine the walls. And the Venetians mounted on the bridges of their ships and hardily assailed the walls and the French likewise assailed them with their engines. When the Greeks saw the French attacking them thus, they set to hurling huge blocks of stone, more than enough, onto the engines of the French, and they began to crush and break to pieces and destroy all these engines, so that no one dared to remain inside or under them. And the Venetians on their part were not able to reach the walls or the towers, they were so high. Nor ever that day were the Venetians or the French able to accomplish anything at the walls or at the city. When they saw that they could not do anything, they were greatly disheartened and drew off. When the Greeks saw them withdrawing, they began to hoot and to call out more lustily than a great deal, and they mounted on the walls and let down their clouts and showed them their backsides. When Murzuphlus saw that the pilgrims had retreated, he began to have his trumpets sounded and his timbrels and to make a din, more than a great deal, and he sent for his people and began to say: "See, lords, am I not a good emperor? Never did you have so good an emperor! Have I not done well? We need fear them no longer. I will have them all hanged and dishonored."

When the pilgrims saw this, they were very angry and very sorrowful, and they returned to the other side of the harbor to their quarters. When the barons had returned and had descended from the ships, they met together and were greatly troubled, and they said that it was for their sins that they were not able to succeed better at the city. Finally the bishops and the clergy of the host consulted together and gave judgment that the battle was a righteous one and that they were right to attack them. For anciently they of the city had been obedient to the law of Rome, but now they were disobedient to it, saying that the law of Rome was worth nothing and that all who believed in it were dogs. And the bishops said that on this account they were right to attack them, and that it was not at all a sin, but rather a righteous deed.

Then it was cried through the camp that all should come to the sermon, Venetians and one and all, on Sunday morning, and they did so. Then the bishops preached throughout the camp, the bishop of Soissons, the bishop of Troyes, the bishop of Halberstadt, Master John Faicete, and the abbot of Loos, and they showed the pilgrims that the battle was righteous, for the others were traitors and murderers and disloyal, since they had murdered their rightful lord, and they were worse than the Jews. And the bishops said that they would assoil all those who should attack them, in the name of God and by the authority of the apostolic. Then the bishops commanded the pilgrims all to confess themselves well and to take communion, and not to be afraid of attacking the Greeks, for they were the enemies of God. And it was commanded that all the light women of the camp be sought out and put out of the camp and sent far away. And so they put them all on a ship and sent them far away from the camp.

Then when the bishops had preached and had shown the pilgrims that the battle was a righteous one, they all confessed themselves right well and were given communion. When it came to Monday morning,[93] the pilgrims all made themselves ready and armed themselves right well, and the Venetians also. Then they repaired the bridges on their ships and got ready

[93] Monday, April 12; the assault was made on the sea walls along the Golden Horn (see map facing p. 31: C).

their transports and their galleys and ranged them side by side
for the assault, and the navy had fully a good league of front.
When they reached the shore and had drawn up as close as they
could to the walls, they cast anchor. And when they were at
anchor, they began to attack vigorously and to shoot and hurl
stones and throw Greek fire on the towers, but the fire could
not take hold on them because of the hides with which they
were covered. And those within the city defended themselves
right hardily, and they had fully sixty petraries hurling missiles, and at each cast they hit the ships, but the ships were so
well covered with planks and with grapevines that they did not
do them any harm, and the stones were so large that a man
could not lift one of them from the ground. And Murzuphlus
was on his mound, and he was making his trumpets sound and
his timbrels and making a great din, and he was encouraging
his people and saying: "Go here! Go there!" and sending them
where he saw there was most need. Now in all the navy there
were not more than four or five ships which could come at the
towers, so high they were. And the wooden towers, which had
been built on top of the stone towers to the height of five or
six or seven stories, were all manned with sergeants to defend
them. So they kept up the attack until by a miracle of God the
ship of the bishop of Soissons [94] struck against one of the towers,
as the sea, which is never still there, carried it forward. Now
on the bridge of this ship there was a Venetian and two armed
knights, and as the ship struck against this tower the Venetian
took hold of it with hands and feet the best he could and got
himself inside. When he was inside, the sergeants who were in
this story—the English, Danes, and Greeks there—looked
around and saw him, and they rushed on him with axes and
swords and cut him to pieces. And as the sea carried the ship
forward again, it struck against this tower again, and as it did

---

[94] The letter of Emperor Baldwin says that the tower was attacked by the
ships of the bishop of Soissons and the bishop of Troyes, the *Paradisus* and
the *Peregrina*, tied together. Villehardouin also mentions these two ships
by name. His account (§§ 242 ff.) tallies remarkably with that of Robert.

so one of the two knights, Andrew of Dureboise[95] was his name, what did he do but take hold of this tower with hands and feet and get himself inside on his knees. When he was inside on his knees, they rushed upon him with axes and swords and struck him fiercely, but, because he was in armor, by God's mercy they did not wound him—as if God were protecting him, because He was not willing that they should hold out longer or that this man should die. Instead, because of their treason and disloyalty and the murder that Murzuphlus had done, He willed that the city should be taken and all the people of the city dishonored. So this knight got to his feet, and as soon as he was on his feet he drew his sword. When they saw him on his feet, they were so astounded and had so great fear that they fled to the next story below, and when those of the next story saw that those above were fleeing, they dared not stay there any longer, but vacated this story also. Then the other knight entered after the first one, and many other people also. And when they were inside they took good ropes and tied this ship strongly to the tower, and when they had it tied a great many people entered. But when the sea carried the ship off again, this tower shook so hard that it seemed as if the ship must surely pull it down, so that perforce and through fear they had to untie the ship. When those of the other stories below saw that the tower was being occupied by the French in this way, they had so great fear that no one dared remain there any longer, but they vacated the whole tower. And Murzuphlus was watching this and he was encouraging his people and sending them to this place where the great assault was being made. While this was happening, this tower being taken by such a miracle, the ship of Lord Pierre of Bracheux struck against another tower, and when it had struck against it, those who were on the bridge of this ship began to attack the tower hardily, until by a miracle of God this tower also was taken.

When these two towers had been taken and manned by our people and they were within the towers, they did not dare move

[95] Villehardouin gives his name as "Andrius d'Ureboise"; one manuscript has "de Tureboise."

from there because of the great multitude of people whom
they saw on the wall near them and in the other towers and
along the foot of the walls, so that it was a fair marvel how
many there were. When my lord Pierre of Amiens saw that
those who were in the towers were not advancing and saw the
condition of the Greeks, what does he do but descend to the
land on foot, he and his people with him, on a little piece of
ground that was between the sea and the wall. When they
were on land, they looked ahead and saw a false postern, the
door of which had been removed and it had been walled up
again. So he came here, and he had with him all of ten knights
and all of sixty sergeants. Now there was a clerk there,
Aleaumes of Clari was his name, who was so doughty in every
need that he was the first in every assault where he was present.
And at the taking of the tower of Galata this clerk did more
deeds of prowess of his own body than any other one of the
host, man for man, save only Lord Pierre of Bracheux. (This
Pierre was the one who surpassed all others, both high and
low, so that there was no one who ever did so many deeds of
arms and of prowess of his own body as did this Pierre of
Bracheux.) When they were come to this postern, they began
to attack it hardily with their picks, and the quarrels of the
crossbows were flying so thick and they were hurling so many
stones down on them from the walls, that it seemed as if they
would be buried under them, so many were thrown. And those
below had shields and targes with which they covered those who
were picking at the postern. And the others hurled down on
them pots full of boiling pitch and Greek fire and immense
stones, so that it was a miracle of God they were not all crushed.
And my lord Pierre of Amiens and his people endured there
labors and difficulties more than a great deal. So they picked
away at this postern with axes and with good swords, with pieces
of wood, with bars and with picks, until they made a great hole
in it. And when this postern was pierced, they looked through
it and saw so many people, both high and low, that it seemed
as if half the world were there, and they did not dare risk
entering in.

When Aleaumes the clerk saw that no one dared enter, he pushed forward and said that he would enter. Now there was a knight there, a brother of his, Robert of Clari was his name, who withstood him and said he should not enter. And the clerk said he would, and he got down on his hands and knees. When his brother saw this, he seized him by the foot and began to pull at him, but finally, in spite of his brother, whether he would or no, the clerk got through. When he was inside, the Greeks ran at him more than a great many, and those on the walls began to throw enormous stones at him. When the clerk saw this, he drew his sword and ran at them and made them flee before him like cattle. And he called to those outside, to Lord Pierre and his people: "Lords, enter hardily! I see them drawing back dismayed and beginning to run away." When my lord Pierre and his people, who were outside, heard this, then my lord Pierre and his people entered in, and he was one of not more than ten knights, but he had all of sixty sergeants with him, and they were all on foot within the walls. Now when they were inside and those who were on the walls and in this quarter saw them, they had such fear that they dared not remain there, but vacated a large part of the wall and fled away, each one as best he could. And the emperor Murzuphlus the traitor was close at hand, less than a stone's throw away, and he was making his silver trumpets sound and his timbrels and making a great din.

When he saw my lord Pierre and his people inside on foot, he made a great show of spurring his horse and riding at him, and he came at least halfway. When my lord Pierre saw him coming, he began encouraging his people, saying: "Now, lords, now to acquit yourselves well! We shall have the battle now, here is the emperor coming. See to it that no one dare to give way, but think only to acquit yourselves well."

When Murzuphlus the traitor saw that they were not going to flee, he halted and then turned back again to his tents. When my lord Pierre saw that the emperor had turned back, he sent a troop of his sergeants to a gate which was near there, and commanded them to break it down and open it. And they went and began to hack and to strike at this gate with axes and swords, until they broke the great iron bolts and bars, and opened the gate. And when the gate was open and those outside saw it, they had their transports brought up and the horses led out, and they mounted and began to enter into the city by this gate at a great rate. Now when the French were inside all mounted and the emperor Murzuphlus the traitor saw them, he had so great fear that he left his tents and his treasures there and fled away back into the city, which was very large and long and wide. For they say that it takes a good nine leagues to go around the walls, so great a circuit have the walls which go around the city, and the city within is all of two French leagues in length and two in breadth. And so it was that my lord Pierre had the tents of Murzuphlus and the coffers and treasures which he had left there. When those who were defending the towers and the walls saw that the French were entered into the city and their emperor had fled away, they did not dare remain there but fled away each one as best he could. Thus was the city taken. When the city was taken in this way and the French were inside, they stayed right where they were. Then the high barons assembled and took counsel among them as to what they should do. And finally it was cried through the host that no one should dare to go on into the city, for it was a great peril to go there, lest they should cast stones on them from the palaces, which were very large and high, or lest they should slay them in the streets, which were so narrow that they would not be able to defend themselves, or lest the city should be set on fire behind them and they be burned. Because of these dangers and perils, they did not dare seek quarters or disperse, but remained there right where they were. Then the barons agreed on this plan, that if the Greeks, who had still a hundred times as many men under arms as the French had, wanted to fight them on the morrow, they would arm themselves on the morrow morning and arrange their forces and await them in an open place which was farther on in the city. And if they would neither fight nor surrender the city, then they would watch from what quarter the wind was blowing, and they would set fire with the wind and burn them out.[96] Thus they would take them by force. All the barons agreed to this plan. When it was come to vespers, the pilgrims disarmed themselves and rested and ate and lay down there that night within the walls in front of their navy.

When it came toward midnight, and the emperor Murzuphlus the traitor knew that all the French were inside the city, he was very much afraid and dared not remain there longer, but fled away at midnight so that no one knew anything about it. When the Greeks saw that their emperor had fled, they took a high man of the city, Lascaris was his name,[97] straightway that very night and made him emperor. When this man was made emperor, he dared not remain there, but he got on a galley before it was day and passed over the Arm of St. George and went off to Nicaea the great, which is a fine city. There he stayed and he was lord and emperor of it.

When morning came on the morrow, what do they do, the priests and clergy in their vestments, the English, Danes, and people of other countries, but come in procession to the camp of the French and cry them mercy and tell them all that the Greeks had done, and they said that all the Greeks had fled and no one was left in the city but the poor people. When the French heard this, they were mightily glad. Then they had it cried through the host that no one should take possession of a house until it had been decided how they should be divided. Then the high men, the rich men, came together and agreed among themselves to take the best houses of the city, without the common people or the poor knights of the host knowing anything about it. And from that time on they began to betray the

[96] In fact, fire did break out in the city that night. Villehardouin says that fire was set to certain buildings by some of the crusaders who feared the Greeks were going to attack them. Gunther says a German count (supposed to be Bertold of Katzenellenbogen) ordered the fire to be set. Villehardouin says that it burned all that night and the next day until vespers and that more houses were burned than would be found in the three largest cities of France. Nicetas says that it burned the quarter along the Golden Horn eastward, from the monastery of Christ the Benefactor to the "quarter of Drungarius," which is more than half a mile away.

[97] Theodore Lascaris, emperor of Nicaea, 1204-22.

common people and to keep bad faith and bad comradeship with them, for which they paid very dearly later, as we shall tell you. So they sent to seize all the best houses and the richest of the city, and they had them all taken before the poor knights and the common people of the host were aware of it. And when the poor people were aware of it, they went each one as best he could and took what they could get. And many they found and many they took and many were left, for the city was very large and populous. And the marquis took possession of the palace of Boukoleon [98] and the church of Saint Sophia, and the houses of the patriarch. And the other high men, like the counts, took possession of the richest palaces and the richest abbeys to be found there. For after the city was taken they did no harm to rich or poor, but those who wanted to go went away and those who wanted to do so stayed, and the richest of the city went away.

Afterwards it was ordered that all the wealth of the spoils should be brought to a certain church in the city. The wealth was brought there, and they took ten knights, high men, of the pilgrims and ten of the Venetians who were thought to be honorable, and they set them to guard this wealth. So the wealth was brought there. And it was so rich, and there were so many rich vessels of gold and silver and cloth of gold and so many rich jewels, that it was a fair marvel, the great wealth that was brought there. Not since the world was made, was there ever seen or won so great a treasure or so noble or so rich, not in the time of Alexander nor in the time of Charlemagne nor before nor after. Nor do I think, myself, that in the forty richest cities of the world there had been so much wealth as was found in Constantinople. For the Greeks say that two thirds of the wealth of this world is in Constantinople and the other third scattered throughout the world.[99] And the very ones who

[98] *Bouke de Lion*; see below, note 100.

[99] Villehardouin (§ 250) uses very similar terms in his effort to convey the immensity of the spoils of Constantinople: "And so much wealth was won there that no one could ever tell you the end of it—of gold and silver and fine vessels and precious stones, of samite and cloth of silk, of fur robes of vaire and grey and ermine, and all the treasures that ever were found on

were to guard the wealth took gold ornaments and whatever else they wanted and robbed the treasure. And each one of the rich men took gold ornaments or cloth of silk and gold or anything else he wanted and carried it off. So in this way they began to rob the treasure, so that nothing was shared with the common people of the host or the poor knights or the sergeants who had helped to win the treasure, save the plain silver, like the silver pitchers which the ladies of the city used to carry to the baths. And the other wealth that remained to be divided was concealed in such evil ways as I have told you. But in any event the Venetians had their half, and the precious stones and the great treasure that remained to be divided went such evil ways as I shall tell you later.

When the city was captured and the pilgrims were quartered, as I have told you, and the palaces were taken over, then they found in the palaces riches more than a great deal. And the palace of Boukoleon was very rich and was made in such a way as I shall tell you. Within this palace, which was held by the marquis, there were fully five hundred halls, all connected with one another and all made with gold mosaic.[100] And in it

---

earth. And Geoffrey of Villehardouin, marshal of Champagne, bears witness of his knowledge and for truth that never since the world was made was so much treasure won in any city." He says that the barons paid from their share 50,000 marks to the Venetians and distributed 100,000 marks among the host, one sergeant on horse receiving as much as two sergeants on foot, and one knight as much as two sergeants on horse. In regard to the booty as a whole, he says that, but for what was stolen and the half that went to the Venetians, the treasure would have been worth fully 400,000 marks of silver and 10,000 suits of armor (*chevaucheures*). How these figures grew in the tales of returning pilgrims is illustrated by the words of Ralph of Coggeshall: "Emperor Baldwin received and distributed to the leaders and the army of the Latins a third of the imperial treasure, amounting to 1,800,000 marks of silver; this immense amount and other things reported about the wealth of the city seem incredible to us."

[100] In these terms Robert attempts to describe the great complex of buildings lying between the Hippodrome and the sea walls, which was known as the Great Palace (map facing p. 31: E). Begun by Constantine, it was added to by later emperors, until the time of the Comneni, who abandoned it for the palace of Blachernae at the other end of the city, which William of Tyre (Bk. II, chap. 7) calls the "New Palace" (D). The Great Palace was occupied again by Andronicus and by Alexius III, as also later by the Latin emperors.

there were fully thirty chapels, great and small, and there was one of them which was called the Holy Chapel,[101] which was so rich and noble that there was not a hinge nor a band nor any other part such as is usually made of iron that was not all of silver, and there was no column that was not of jasper or porphyry or some other rich precious stone. And the pavement of this chapel was of a white marble so smooth and clear that it seemed to be of crystal, and this chapel was so rich and so noble that no one could ever tell you its great beauty and nobility. Within this chapel were found many rich relics. One found there two pieces of the True Cross as large as the leg of a man and as long as half a *toise*, and one found there also the iron of the lance with which Our Lord had His side pierced and two of the nails which were driven through His hands and feet, and one found there in a crystal phial quite a little of His blood, and one found there the tunic which He wore and which was taken from Him when they led Him to the Mount of Calvary, and one found there the blessed crown with which He was crowned, which was made of reeds with thorns as sharp as the points of daggers.[102] And one found there a part of the robe of Our Lady and the head of my lord St. John the Baptist and so many other rich relics that I could not recount them to you or tell you all the truth.

See the remarkable study by Ebersolt, *Le Grand Palais*, with plan. The name Boukoleon was originally used by the Greeks for a small palace just above the harbor of that name. According to Anna Comnena (*Alexias*, III, 1), this name was taken from a sculptured group on the quay of the harbor, representing a struggle between a bull and a lion. The name was taken in the West to mean "Lion's mouth"; hence Villehardouin's *Boche de Lion*, Robert's *Bouke de Lion*, and Rigord's *Os leonis*.

[101] This is the celebrated church of the Blessed Virgin of the Pharos (lighthouse). It was begun by Constantine V Copronymous (741-55) and completed by Michael III (842-67) and was included in the group of buildings composing the Great Palace. Robert's list of relics preserved in this church is strikingly confirmed by the account of Anthony of Novgorod, who made a pilgrimage to Constantinople about 1200, and who refers to it as "a little church of the Blessed Virgin" in the "imperial Golden Palace" (*Itinéraires russes*, I, i, 98).

[102] For the history of the Crown of Thorns, see de Mély, *Exuviae*, pp. 165 ff.

Now there was still another relic in this chapel which we had forgotten to tell you about. For there were two rich vessels of gold hanging in the midst of the chapel by two heavy silver chains. In one of these vessels there was a tile and in the other a cloth. And we shall tell you where these relics came from. There was once a holy man in Constantinople. It happened that this holy man was covering the house of a widow with tile for the love of God. And as he was covering it, Our Lord appeared to him and said to him (now this good man had a cloth wrapped about him): "Give me that cloth," said Our Lord. And the good man gave it to Him, and Our Lord enveloped His face with it so that His features were imprinted on it. And then He handed it back to him, and He told him to carry it with him and touch the sick with it, and whoever had faith in it would be healed of his sickness. And the good man took it and carried it away; but before he carried it away, after God had given him back his cloth, the good man took it and hid it under a tile until vespers. At vespers, when he went away, he took the cloth, and as he lifted up the tile, he saw the image imprinted on the tile just as it was on the cloth, and he carried the tile and the cloth away, and afterwards he cured many sick with them.[108] And these relics were hanging in the midst of the

[108] This is a variant of the legend of the "Image of Edessa," or the "Portrait not made by hand of man." The official version is found in the entry for August 19 in the Synaxary, or church calendar, of Constantinople (edited by Delehaye in the *Acta sanctorum: Propylaeum ad acta sanctorum Novembris*). This commemorates the bringing of the picture from Edessa to Constantinople by Emperor Romanus in 944. In 968 Constantinople secured the tile with the image imprinted on it, and in 1032 the autograph letter. The latter, however, was destroyed in the sack of the palace in 1185. The legend is as follows: King Abgar of Edessa, afflicted with an incurable disease, sent an envoy to Jesus to ask Him to come to Edessa and cure him. The envoy was instructed to make a portrait of Jesus, but when he arrived and had washed his hands, Jesus took the cloth and put it to His face and gave it back with the divine features imprinted on it. The envoy returned with the miraculous portrait and with a letter to the king written by the hand of Jesus. On the way back occurred the incident of the hiding of the towel under a tile and the transfer of the image to the tile. The origin and growth of the legend are admirably traced by Tixeront (*Les Origines de l'église d'Édesse et la légende d'Abgar*); see also the two articles by

chapel, as I have told you. Now there was in this chapel still
another relic, for there was an image of St. Demetrius which
was painted on a panel.[104] This image gave off so much oil that
it could not be removed as fast as it flowed from the picture.[105]
[And there was another palace in the city, called the palace of
Blachernae.] And there were fully twenty chapels there and at
least two hundred chambers, or three hundred, all connected with
one another and all made of gold mosaic. And this palace was so
rich and so noble that no one could describe it to you or recount
its great nobility and richness. In this palace of Blachernae there
was found a very great treasure, for one found there the rich
crowns which had belonged to former emperors and the rich
ornaments of gold and the rich cloth of silk and gold and the
rich imperial robes and the rich precious stones and so many
other riches that no one could number the great treasure of
gold and silver that was found in the palaces and in many other
places in the city.

Then the pilgrims regarded the great size of the city, and
the palaces and fine abbeys and churches and the great wonders
which were in the city, and they marveled at it greatly. And
they marveled greatly at the church of Saint Sophia and at the
riches which were in it.

LeClercq, "Abgar," and "Édesse," in Cabrol's *Dictionnaire d'archéologie
chrétienne*. Runciman ("Some Remarks on the Image of Edessa," *Cambridge
Historical Journal*, 1931, pp. 232-52) identifies it with the *sanctam toellam*
listed in the charter of Baldwin II by which he transferred to Louis IX the
title to the relics which the latter had acquired. It was apparently destroyed
in the sack of the Sainte Chapelle in 1792.

[104] The church of the great martyr St. Demetrius was founded by Basil I
(867-86). It is just north of the church of the Virgin (Robert's "Holy
Chapel") and is connected with it by a vestibule, so that Robert speaks of it
as part of the same building. Oil from the portrait of this saint is referred
to in a deed issued by the chaplain of Emperor Baldwin to the church of St.
John of Soissons (Riant, *Exuviae*, II, 61 f.). Anna Comnena (Bk. II, 8)
and Nicetas (p. 397) both speak of oil from the sarcophagus of the saint in
Thessalonica. Emperor Manuel brought the portrait from this city to Constantinople and placed it in the church of the Pantocrator.

[105] As Pauphilet (*loc. cit.*, p. 307) points out, the copyist has evidently
omitted here a sentence introducing the subject of the palace of Blachernae,
which Robert describes in the following sentences.

Now I will tell you about the church of Saint Sophia, how it was made. Saint Sophia in Greek means Sainte Trinité ["Holy Trinity"] in French [*sic*]. The church of Saint Sophia was entirely round, and within the church there were domes, round all about, which were borne by great and very rich columns, and there was no column which was not of jasper or porphyry or some other precious stone, nor was there one of these columns that did not work cures. There was one that cured sickness of the reins when it was rubbed against, and another that cured sickness of the side, and others that cured other ills.[106] And there was no door in this church and no hinges or bands or other parts such as are usually made of iron that were not all of silver. The master altar of the church was so rich that it was beyond price, for the table of the altar was made of gold and precious stones broken up and crushed all together, which a rich emperor had had made. This table was fully fourteen feet long. Around the altar were columns of silver supporting a canopy over the altar which was made just like a church spire, and it was all of solid silver and was so rich that no one could tell the money it was worth. The place where they read the gospel was so fair and noble that we could not describe to you how it was made. Then down through the church there hung fully a hundred chandeliers, and there was not one that did not hang by a great silver chain as thick as a man's arm. And there were in each chandelier full five and twenty lamps or more. And there was not a chandelier that was not worth at least two hundred marks of silver. On the ring of the great door of the church, which was all of silver, there hung a tube,[107] of what material no one knew; it was the size of a pipe such as shepherds play on. This tube had such virtue as I shall tell you. When an

[106] Anthony of Novgorod (*Itinéraires russes*, I, i, 90) tells of the healing properties of the column of St. Gregory the Thaumaturge in Saint Sophia.

[107] *buhotiaus*; derivation and meaning uncertain. Pauphilet (*loc. cit.*, pp. 308 ff.) considers it a diminutive of *buhot*, "spout of a vessel," and has an ingenious explanation: it may have been a tube connected with an air pump by means of which the priests of Saint Sophia worked the miracle. Anthony of Novgorod (*loc. cit.*, p. 91) calls it a "romaniston, that is, a bolt with which the portal was fastened." He tells a similar tale of its miraculous powers.

infirm man who had some sickness in his body like the bloat, so that he was bloated in his belly, put it in his mouth, however little he put it in, when this tube took hold it sucked out all the sickness and it made the poison run out of his mouth and it held him so fast that it made his eyes roll and turn in his head, and he could not get away until the tube had sucked all of this sickness out of him. And the sicker a man was the longer it held him, and if a man who was not sick put it in his mouth, it would not hold him at all, much or little.

Then in front of this church of Saint Sophia there was a great column which was fully three times the reach of a man's arms in thickness and was fully fifty *toises* in height. It was made of marble and of copper over the marble and was bound about with strong bands of iron. And on top of this column there lay a flat slab of stone which was fully fifteen feet in length and as much in width. On this stone there was an emperor made of copper on a great copper horse, and he was holding out his hand toward heathendom, and there were letters written on the statue which said that he swore that the Saracens should never have truce from him. And in the other hand he held a golden globe with a cross on it. The Greeks said that this was Heraclius the emperor.[108] And on the croup of the horse and on the head and round about there were fully ten nests of herons, who nested there every year.

Then elsewhere in the city there was another church which

---

[108] This was in fact the equestrian statue of Emperor Justinian in the Forum of the Augusteion, which lies between Saint Sophia and the entrance to the Great Palace (map facing p. 31: 3). See Diehl, *Justinian*, pp. 77 ff., and especially Ebersolt, *Constantinople byzantine*, pp. 28 ff. The descriptions confirm Robert's testimony to a remarkable degree. The survival of the statue through the fourteenth and fifteenth centuries is attested by the accounts of several visitors to Constantinople: Stephen of Novgorod about 1350, John Schiltzberger of Munich, the Florentine Buondelmonti, and the Frenchman Bertrandon, all three early in the fifteenth century. Peter Gilles, who was in Constantinople about 1550, gives a vivid description, but says that the statue had been thrown down from its base some thirty years before (*Petri Gylii de topographia Constantinopoleos ... libri quatuor*, II, xvii, 103 f.). He asserts that he saw fragments of the bronze of gigantic proportions still waiting to be melted down to make cannon.

was called the church of the Seven Apostles.[109] And it was said to be even richer and nobler than the church of Saint Sophia. There was so much richness and nobility there that no one could recount to you the richness and nobility of this church. And there lay in this church the bodies of seven apostles. There was also the marble column to which Our Lord was bound, before He was put on the cross. And it was said that Constantine the emperor lay there and Helena [Constantine's mother], and many other emperors.

Now there was elsewhere in the city a gate which was called the Golden Mantle.[110] On this gate there was a golden globe which was made by such enchantment that the Greeks said as long as it was there no thunderbolt would fall in the city. On this globe there was an image cast of copper, with a golden mantle clasped about it, which it held out on its arm, and it had letters written on it which said: "Anyone," said the image, "who lives in Constantinople a year can have a golden mantle just as I have."

Elsewhere in the city there is another gate which is called the Golden Gate.[111] On this gate there were two elephants made of

[109] *Set apostres*; perhaps an error for *Saints Apostres*. This is the church of the Holy Apostles. It contained the relics of one apostle (St. Andrew), not seven, and also the relics of St. Luke and St. Timothy. This famous church was built by Justinian on the site of an older church of the Apostles built by Constantine; it was the model for St. Mark's of Venice. See Heisenberg, *Grabeskirche und Apostelkirche*, pp. 188 ff., with plans. Richter (*Quellen*, pp. 101 ff.) gives the list of the emperors and empresses whose tombs were in this church, with references to the sources. Anthony of Novgorod mentions the column of flagellation preserved there. See also Vasiliev, *Byzantine Empire*, I, 229.

[110] Hopf (*Chroniques gréco-romanes*, p. 68, note 2) identifies this as the Gate of the Gyrolimné, the gate in the wall immediately in front of the Palace of Blachernae, but his identification is doubtful. Of the Gate of the Gyrolimné, Van Millingen says (*Byzantine Constantinople*, p. 127) that the arch was decorated with three imperial busts.

[111] The most famous gate of the city, located near the southern end of the land walls (see map facing p. 31). Van Millingen (*loc. cit.*, pp. 59 ff.) suggests that it was originally the triumphal arch erected by Theodosius I to celebrate his victory over Maximus, sometime between 388 and 391, before the walls of Theodosius II were built. He cites Cedrenus as mentioning a bronze group of four elephants on this gate. Its use as a triumphal entry is

copper which were so large that it was a fair marvel. This gate was never opened except when an emperor was returning from battle after conquering territory. And when an emperor returned from battle after conquering territory, then the clergy of the city would come out in procession to meet him, and the gate would be opened, and they would bring out a chariot of gold, which was made like a cart with four wheels, such as we call a *curre*. Now in the middle of this chariot there was a high seat and on the seat there was a throne and around the throne there were four columns which bore a canopy to shade the throne, which seemed as if it were all of gold. Then the emperor, wearing his crown, would take his seat on the throne, and he would enter through this gate and be borne in this chariot, with great joy and rejoicing, to his palace.

Now in another part of the city there was another marvel. There was an open place near the palace of Boukoleon which was called the Games of the Emperor.[112] This place was a good bowshot and a half long and nearly a bowshot wide. Around this place there were fully thirty rows of seats or forty, on which the Greeks used to mount to watch the games, and above these rows there was a loge, very dainty and very noble, where the emperor and the empress sat when the games were held, and the other high men and ladies. And if there were two sides playing at the same time, the emperor and the empress would wager with each other that one side would play better than the other, and so would all the others who watched the games. Along this open place there was a wall which was a good fifteen feet high and ten feet wide. Upon this wall there were figures of men and women, and of horses and oxen and camels and bears and lions and many other kinds of animals, all made of copper, and all so well made and formed so naturally that there is no master workman in heathendom or in Christendom

attested by many events in Byzantine history. See Strzygowski, "Das goldne Thor in Konstantinopel," *Jahrbuch d. kaiserlich-deutschen arch. Instituts*, VIII, 1-39.
[112] *Jus l'empereur*; the Hippodrome; see map facing p. 31: 4.

so skillful as to be able to make figures as good as these.[113] And formerly they used to play by enchantment, but they do not play any longer. And the French looked at the Games of the Emperor in wonder when they saw it.

Now there was elsewhere in the city another marvel. There were two statues made of copper in the form of women, well and naturally made, and more beautiful than a good deal. And neither of them was less than a good twenty feet in height. One of these figures held its hand out toward the West, and it had letters written on it which said: "From the West will come those who will capture Constantinople," and the other figure held its hand out toward a vile place and said: "Here," said the figure, "here is where they will throw them." [114] These two figures were sitting in front of the Change, which used to be very rich there, for the rich money changers used to be there with great heaps of besants and of precious stones in front of them, before the city was taken, but there were not so many of them afterwards.

There was elsewhere in the city still another great marvel. There were two columns, each of them at least three times the reach of a man's arms in thickness and at least fifty *toises* in height. And hermits used to live on the tops of these columns in little shelters that were there, and there were doors [115] in the columns by which one could ascend. On the outside of these columns there were pictured and written by prophecy all the events and all the conquests which have happened in Constantinople or which were going to happen. But no one could

[113] Ebersolt (*Constantinople byzantine*, pp. 33 f.) quotes the eleventh-century Arabian geographer Edrisi as saying of the Hippodrome that one walks between two rows of bronze statues representing men and bears and lions, larger than life in size.

[114] Nicetas (pp. 739 f.) describes a magnificent bronze statue of Athena which the mob overturned and destroyed during the siege. The left hand held back the draperies while the right supported the head which was slightly inclined toward the south. Those who did not know the directions declared that the statue was looking toward the West and inviting with its hand the army of the West to attack the city.

[115] The manuscript reads *huis*, "door," which Jeanroy (*loc. cit.*) would amend to read *vis*, "spiral staircase."

understand the event until it had happened, and when it had happened the people would go there and ponder over it, and then for the first time they would see and understand the event. And even this conquest of the French was written and pictured there and the ships in which they made the assault when the city was taken, and the Greeks were not able to understand it before it had happened, but when it had happened they went to look at these columns and ponder over it, and they found that the letters which were written on the pictured ships said that a people, short haired [116] and with iron swords, would come from the West to conquer Constantinople.[117] All these marvels which I

[116] *haut tondue.*

[117] According to Ebersolt (*Constantinople byzantine*, p. 40), these were the columns of Theodosius the Great in the Forum of Theodosius (the Tauros), erected in 386, and of Arcadius in the Forum of the Xerolophos, erected in 403 (see map facing p. 31: 5, 6). They were modeled on the column of Trajan in Rome. See the study by Strzygowski, "Die Säule des Arkadius" (*Jahrbuch d. kaiserlich-deutschen arch. Inst.*, VIII, 230-49), with references to Du Cange, Banduri, Gilles, and other older writers who had described Constantinople. On the basis of the figures given by Gilles, he estimates the height of the column of Arcadius as 47 meters, or over 150 feet. In describing the column from the top of which Murzuphlus was thrown, both Villehardouin and Gunther speak of the sculptured figures with which it was covered. Gunther says that the sculptures were believed to represent the prophecies of the Sibyl, and included ships with ladders and men on the ladders ascending to assault the city. When the people of Constantinople saw the ladders erected on the Venetian ships, they recognized the warning of the sculptures and mutilated them with stones and hammers, in order to bring bad luck upon the invaders. Villehardouin says that the sculptures included the figure of a man in the garb of an emperor and he was falling down, for it had been prophesied from a long time back that an emperor of Constantinople would be thrown from this column. The populace of Constantinople seems to have had a special fondness for fateful prophecies. Ralph of Diceto (*anno* 1189) cites the supposed letter of the envoys whom Philip Augustus sent to Constantinople (this letter was probably a fabrication, since the substance of it is also found in a letter attributed by Roger of Wendover to Conrad of Montferrat), in which it was reported that an old Greek told Walter the Templar that the Latins would conquer Constantinople, because it was written on the Golden Gate, which had not been opened for two hundred years: "When the blond king of the West shall come, I will open of myself." Nicetas says that at the approach of the army of Frederick Barbarossa a monk prophesied that he would enter the city by a certain gate, and Isaac had the gate walled up. Ralph of Coggeshall has a

have recounted to you here and still a great many more than
we could recount, the French found in Constantinople after
they had captured it, nor do I think, for my part, that any
man on earth [118] could number all the abbeys of the city, so
many there were, both of monks and of nuns, aside from the
other churches outside of the city. And it was reckoned that
there were in the city a good thirty thousand priests, both
monks and others. Now about the rest of the Greeks, high and
low, rich and poor, about the size of the city, about the palaces
and the other marvels that are there, we shall leave off telling
you. For no man on earth, however long he might have lived
in the city, could number them or recount them to you. And if
anyone should recount to you the hundredth part of the richness and the beauty and the nobility that was found in the
abbeys and in the churches and in the palaces and in the city,
it would seem like a lie and you would not believe it. And
among the rest, there was another of the churches which they
called My Lady Saint Mary of Blachernae, where was kept the
sydoine in which Our Lord had been wrapped, which stood up
straight every Friday so that the features of Our Lord could be
plainly seen there.[119] And no one, either Greek or French, ever
knew what became of this *sydoine* after the city was taken.
And there was another of the abbeys where the good emperor
Manuel lay, and never was anyone born on this earth, sainted
man or sainted woman, who was so richly and so nobly
sepulchred as was this emperor. In this abbey there was the
marble slab on which Our Lord was laid when He was taken

story of an inscription on a column in Constantinople which said that after
three emperors named Alexius the rule of the Greeks would end and the
empire would be transferred to a foreign people.

[118] *nus hons conterres*; the last word may mean "counter, reckoner," but
more likely "on earth," like *nus homes terriens* below.

[119] Robert seems to have confused the *sudarium* (the sweat cloth or napkin,
the True Image of St. Veronica) with the *sindon* (the grave cloth in which
the body of Jesus was wrapped for entombment). Both relics were in the
church of the Blessed Virgin in the Great Palace, and not in the church in the
palace of Blachernae, as Robert says. The confusion between *sudarium* and
sindon is found also in the charter of Baldwin II of 1247 (see note 89):
partem sudarii quo involutum fuit corpus eius in sepulchro.

When they had crowned him, they seated him on a high throne, and he was there while the mass was sung, and he held in one hand his scepter and in the other hand a golden globe with a cross on it. And the jewels which he was wearing were worth more than the treasure of a rich king would make. When the mass was heard, they brought him a white horse on which he mounted. Then the barons took him back to his palace of Boukoleon and seated him on the throne of Constantine. Then when he was seated on the throne of Constantine, they all did homage to him as emperor and all the Greeks who were there bowed down before him as the sacred emperor. Then the tables were placed and the emperor ate and all the barons with him in the palace. When they had eaten, the barons all departed and went to their houses and the emperor remained in his palace.

Afterwards it came about one day that the barons assembled and said among them that the wealth should be divided, but none of it was divided then save the common silver that was there, such as the silver pitchers which the ladies of the city used to carry to the baths. And they gave some to each knight, to each mounted sergeant, and to all the common people of the host, even to the women and the children, to each one something. Then Aleaumes of Clari, the clerk, of whom I have spoken to you before, who was so worthy in his own person and who did so many feats of arms, as we have told you before, said that he wanted to share as a knight.[125] And some said that it was not right that he should share as a knight, and he said it was, because he had had a horse and a hauberk like any knight and had done as many feats of arms as any knight that was there, and more too. And finally the count of St. Pol gave judgment that he should share as a knight, because he had done more deeds of arms and of prowess, as the count of St.

---

scription of the robes worn by Manuel I at the reception of Kilidj-Arslan in 1161—a great purple robe encrusted with carbuncles and pearls, and on his breast an enormous ruby the size of an apple.

[125] According to the *Devastatio* the clergy were ranked with the sergeants on horse and were to receive 10 marks apiece while the knights received 20.

Pol himself bore witness, than any one of three hundred
knights had done, and for that he ought to share as a knight.
Thus did this clerk prove that the clerks should share just like
the knights. Then all the common silver was divided, as I have
told you, but the other treasures, the gold, the cloth of silk, of
which there was so much that it was a fair marvel, remained
undivided, and it was placed in the common guard of the host,
in the guard of such people as it was thought would guard it
loyally.

It was not long afterwards that the emperor sent for all the
high barons and the doge of Venice and Count Louis and the
count of St. Pol and all the high men, and said he wanted to
go and conquer some of the land, and they decided who should
go with the emperor and who should stay to guard the city.
And it was decided that the doge of Venice should stay and
Count Louis and some of their people with them. And the
marquis stayed and he married the wife of Isaac, the former
emperor, who was sister to the king of Hungary. When the
marquis saw that the emperor was about to go and conquer
the land, he came and asked him to give him the kingdom of
Salonika,[126] a land which was fully fifteen days' journey from
Constantinople. And the emperor answered him that it was not
his to give, for the barons of the host and the Venetians had
the larger part of it. As far as it rested with him he would give
it him very gladly and with great good will, but the part belonging to the barons of the host and to the Venetians he could
not give him. When the marquis saw that he could not have it,
he was in a great rage. Then the emperor went away where
he had planned to go, with all his people. And as he came to
the castles and the cities, they were yielded to him without
resistance, and the keys were brought out to him, and the priests
and the clerks came in their vestments in procession to meet and
welcome him, and all the Greeks worshipped him as the sacred
emperor. And the emperor placed his guards in the castles and
the cities everywhere as he came to them. And so he conquered
much of the land up to fifteen days' journey from Constanti-

[126] Ancient Thessalonica.

nople, until he came within a day's journey of Salonika. In the meantime, while the emperor was thus conquering the land, the marquis had set out with his wife and all his people to follow after the emperor and he came up with the host of the emperor before the emperor came to Salonika. And when he was come up with the host, he went and encamped a good league on this side, and when he had made camp, he took messengers and sent them to the emperor, and sent word to him not to go into his land of Salonika, that had been given to him. For he should know well that if he went there he would not go with him any longer and would not hold to him longer, but rather he would go back to Constantinople and do the best he could for himself.

When the barons of the emperor's company heard this message which the marquis had sent him, they were greatly enraged and aggrieved. And they sent back word again to the marquis that they would not leave off going, not for him nor for his message, nor for anything at all, for the land was not his.

When the marquis heard this, he turned back and came to a city in which the emperor had placed some of his people as guards, and he took it by treason. When he had taken this city, he placed guards of his own people there. And then when he had done this, he came to another city, Adrianople was its name, in which the emperor had placed some of his people, and he besieged it and had his petraries and mangonels set up to assault the city, and they of the city held out well against him. And when he saw that he could not take them by force, he spoke to those who were on the walls and said to them: "How now, lords? Do you not know that this woman was the wife of Isaac the emperor?" And he brought his wife forward and his wife said: "How now? Do you not recognize me to be the empress, and do you not recognize my two children whom I had of Isaac the emperor?" And she brought forward her children, and finally a wise man of the city made answer: "Yes," he said, "we know well that this was the wife of Isaac the emperor and that these are his children." "Well, then," said the marquis, "why do you not recognize one of the children as your lord?"

"I will tell you," said the man. "Do you go now to Constantinople and have him crowned, and when he has sat on the throne of Constantine and we know of it, then we will do what we ought to."

In the meantime, while the marquis was doing these things, the emperor went on to Salonika and besieged it. And when he had besieged it the host was so impoverished that there was not bread enough to feed more than a hundred men, but they had plenty of flesh and wine. The emperor had not maintained the siege very long before they surrendered the city to him, and after the city was surrendered there was plenty of what was needed, bread and wine and flesh. Then the emperor placed his guards there, and then he decided not to go farther, but instead he turned about to go back to Constantinople.

Then there came upon the host a very great loss and sorrow, for my lord Pierre of Amiens, the fair and the worthy, died on the way back, at a city called La Blanche, which was close to Philippi, where Alexander was born. And fully fifty knights died on this march. Now while the emperor was returning, he heard the news that the marquis had taken one of his cities by treason and had placed his own people in it as guards and had laid siege to Adrianople.

When the emperor and the barons of the host heard this, they were enraged and afflicted more than a great deal, and they threatened the marquis and his people that if they should come up with them they would cut them all to pieces and not leave him alive. When the marquis knew that the emperor was coming back, he was very greatly afraid, as one who had committed a great wrong, so that he scarcely knew what to do. Finally he sent word to Constantinople to the doge of Venice and to Count Louis and to the other barons who had remained there, that he would put himself under their protection and would make amends through them for the wrong he had done. Now when the doge and the count and the other barons heard that the marquis was willing to make amends through them for the wrong he had done, they sent four envoys to the emperor, and they told him that the marquis had appealed to them in this way, and warned him that he was not to do any harm to him or to his people.[127]

When the barons and the knights of the host heard this, they answered that this availed nothing to keep them from dishonoring the marquis and his people and from cutting them all to pieces, if they could come up with them. At length and with great difficulty they were appeased, and in the end they granted the marquis a truce. Then the barons asked the envoys for news of Constantinople and what was being done there. And the envoys answered that things were going very well, and that they had divided the treasure that had remained and the city. "How now?" said the knights and the young bachelors of the host, "You have divided up our treasure for which we have borne the great pains and the great labors, the hunger and the thirst and the cold and the heat, and you have divided it up without us?" "Hold!" said they to the envoys. "Here is my gage," said one, "that I will prove you all to be traitors!" Another thrust himself forward and said the same, and others also, and they were so greatly enraged that they wanted to cut all the envoys to pieces; and for little they would have slain them. Finally the emperor and the high men of the host took counsel and reasoned with them and made peace the best they could, so that they came back together to Constantinople. And when they were returned, there was no one of them who could recover his own house, for the houses from which they had departed were not theirs any longer, because the city had been divided up, and their followers had taken lodging elsewhere in the city, so that it was necessary for them to seek houses a

[127] According to Villehardouin (§§ 288-99) it was the leaders in Constantinople who decided to intervene and compel the parties to accept arbitration. Villehardouin and Manasses of Lisle were sent as their envoys to the marquis, then in front of Adrianople. The marquis agreed to accept as arbiters, the doge, Count Louis of Blois, Conon of Béthune, and Villehardouin. On their return to Constantinople, the leaders sent envoys to Emperor Baldwin, then hastening with his army to attack the marquis. The emperor agreed to abandon the attack and come to Constantinople to consult with the others, and finally peace was made.

good league or two away from those from which they had departed.

Now we had forgotten to tell of an adventure that befell my lord Pierre of Bracheux. It happened that the emperor Henry was on a campaign and John the Vlach and the Comans had raided the land of the emperor, and they were encamped two leagues or less away from the camp of the emperor. Now they had heard much said of my lord Pierre of Bracheux and of his good chivalry, and finally they sent word one day to my lord Pierre of Bracheux by messengers that they would like very much to talk with him some time under safe conduct. My lord Pierre answered that if he had safe conduct he would gladly go and talk with them. So finally the Vlachs and Comans sent good hostages to the camp of the emperor to be held against the safe return of my lord Pierre. Then my lord Pierre mounted a great horse and set off, along with three other knights. As he came near the army of the Vlachs and John the Vlach knew that he was coming, he went out to meet him and some of the high men of Vlachia along with him. They greeted him and gave him welcome and looked at him with great interest, for he was very tall. And they talked with him about one thing and another, until finally they said to him: "Lord, we marvel greatly at your good chivalry, and also we wonder greatly what you are seeking in this country, and why you are coming here to conquer land from so distant a country. Have you not," said they, "any lands in your own country to support you?" And my lord Pierre answered: "How now!" said he. "Have you not heard how Troy the great was destroyed and by what trick?" "Oh yes!" said the Vlachs and the Comans. "We have indeed heard it told, but that was a long time ago." "Well," said Pierre, "Troy belonged to our ancestors and those who escaped from it came and settled in the country we come from; and because it belonged to our ancestors, we are come here to conquer land." With that he took his leave and went back to the camp.[128]

---

[128] It is curious to find this legend of the Trojan origin of the Franks turning up in Robert's chronicle. The legend is found in Rigord's life of

When the emperor and the barons who had gone with him were come back, after conquering a great part of the land and fully sixty cities, besides the castles and villages, then the city of Constantinople was divided, so that the emperor had the fourth part of it in full ownership, and the other three parts were divided so that the Venetians had one half of the three parts and the pilgrims the other. And then they decided to divide the land which had been conquered. And they gave land first to the counts and then afterwards to the other high men. And they considered who was the richest man and the highest and who had had the most people of his own following in the host, and to him they gave the most land. And so to one was given two hundred knights' fiefs, to another a hundred, to another seventy, to another sixty, to another forty, to another twenty, and to another ten; and those who had the least had seven or six of them, and the fief was worth three hundred livres of Anjou. And each one of the high men was told: "You will have so many fiefs, and you so many, and you so many; and you will give the fiefs to your men and to others who are willing to hold from you. And you will have this city, and you that, and you this other, and the seigniories that are attached thereto." When each one had been given his part in this way, the counts and the high men went to see their lands and their cities, and they placed their bailiffs and guards in them.

Now it happened one day that my lord Thierri, brother of the count of Loos, was going to see his land. And as he was going along, in a defile, he came by chance upon Murzuphlus the traitor, who was going I know not where. And he had in his company ladies and maidens and many other people, and he was riding along daintily and nobly like an emperor, with as many people as he could. And what did my lord Thierri do but ride at him, and he and his men succeeded in taking him

Philip Augustus, chaps. 37, 38 (*Œuvres de Rigord*, I, 54 ff.). The fact that this incident is out of place in the narrative (since it must have occurred after Henry became emperor) is used by Wanner to establish the date of dictation of the main part of the chronicle. He supposes that Robert heard of it while he was dictating his story in 1207, and inserted it right away. in the wrong place! See note 9 to the Introduction.

him,[131] and Count Louis and many other high men, and so
many others that we do not know the number of them, but fully
three hundred knights were lost there. And those who escaped
came fleeing to Constantinople, and the doge of Venice came
fleeing and many people with him, and they left their tents
and their harness just as they were when they were encamped
before this city, because they never dared turn that way, so
great was the rout. And thus truly did God take vengeance on
them for their pride and for the bad faith which they had kept
with the poor people of the host, and for the terrible sins which
they had committed in the city after they had taken it.

When the emperor was lost by this disaster, the barons who
were left were greatly dismayed. Afterwards they assembled
one day to choose an emperor, and they sent for my lord
Henry, the brother of the emperor Baldwin who was, to make
him emperor, and he was in his land which he had conquered
beyond the Arm of St. George.

When the doge of Venice and the Venetians saw that they
wanted to make my lord Henry emperor, they were against it,
nor would they suffer it unless they should have a certain image
of Our Lady which was painted on a panel. This image was
rich beyond measure and was all covered with rich precious
stones. And the Greeks said that it was the first image of Our
Lady that was ever made or painted. The Greeks had such
faith in this image that they treasured it above everything, and
they bore it every Sunday in procession; and they worshipped
it and gave great gifts to it. Now the Venetians were not willing to allow my lord Henry to be emperor, unless they should
have this image, so the image was given to them and then my
lord Henry was crowned emperor.[132]

---

[131] Gerland (*Geschichte des lateinischen Kaiserreiches*, I, 91 ff.) discusses
the fate of Emperor Baldwin, who was apparently kept as a hostage at first
and then, later in 1205, slain by Joannissa in a fit of rage.

[132] This was the famous portrait of the Virgin, supposed to have been
painted by the hand of St. Luke. Robert is evidently not well informed
about the events that happened in Constantinople after his own return. The
affair of the icon arose between the Venetians of Constantinople and the
patriarch and canons of the church of St. Sophia some time after the corona-

When my lord Henry was emperor, then they talked together, he and the marquis who was king of Salonika, until the marquis gave him his daughter and the emperor married her. And the empress did not live very long, but died soon afterwards.

It was not long after this that John the Vlach and the Comans rode into the land of the marquis of Salonika. And the marquis was in his land and finally he fought with these Vlachs and Comans, and he was slain in this battle and all his people were defeated. Then John the Vlach and these Comans went and besieged Salonika and had their engines set up to assault the city. And the wife of the marquis had remained in the city, and knights and other people with her to defend the city. Now there lay in this city the body of my lord St. Demetrius, who would never suffer his city to be taken by force. And there flowed from this holy body such great quantities of oil that it was a fair marvel. And it came to pass, as John the Vlach was lying one morning in his tent, that my lord St. Demetrius came and struck him with a lance through the body and slew him. When his own people and the Comans knew that he was dead, they broke camp and went away to their land. And then afterwards the kingdom of Vlachia fell to a nephew of John, Boris was his name. So this Boris became king of Vlachia, and he had a beautiful daughter. Then it happened that the emperor Henry, who was a right good emperor, took counsel with his barons as to what he should do about these Vlachs and Comans, who were thus making war on the empire of Constantinople, and who had slain the emperor Baldwin, his brother. Finally the barons advised him to send to this Boris, who was king of Vlachia, and ask him to give him his daughter to wife.[133] The emperor answered that he would never take a

tion of Emperor Henry. The letter of Innocent III of January 13, 1207 (Potthast, *Regesta*, I, 254, no. 2981; Migne, *Pat. lat.*, CCXV, col. 1077 ff.) tells of the taking of the icon from St. Sophia by the Venetians and its transfer to their own church of the Pantocrator.

[133] The Bulgarian princess whom Emperor Henry married as his second wife was in fact the cousin and not the daughter of Boris; she was the daughter of Joannissa. See Muralt, p. 306.

wife of such low lineage. And the barons said: "Sire, you should do so. We urge you to make peace with them, for they are the most powerful people and the most dread enemy of the empire and of the land." The barons talked so much that the emperor finally sent two knights, high men, and he had them very finely arrayed. The messengers went very fearfully to this savage land, and when they came there the people wanted to slay them. Nevertheless, the messengers talked with this Boris and he replied that he would gladly send his daughter to the emperor.

Then Boris the king had his daughter attired very richly and very nobly, and many people with her. And he sent her to the emperor, and he commanded sixty pack horses to be sent to him all loaded with treasure, with gold and silver and cloth of silk and precious jewels, and there was no horse that was not covered with a cloth of vermilion samite, so long that it trailed behind fully seven or eight feet, and never did they go through mud or by evil roads, so that not one of the samite cloths was injured, all for daintiness and nobility.

When the emperor knew that the maiden was coming, he went to meet her, and the barons with him, and they made great welcome for her and her people, and then afterwards the emperor married her.

It was not a great while afterwards that they sent for the emperor to come to Salonika and crown the son of the marquis as king, and the emperor went there. And when he had crowned the son of the marquis, he fell sick and died there, which was a very great loss and a very great sorrow.

Now you have heard the truth how Constantinople was conquered, and how the count of Flanders, Baldwin, was emperor of it, and my lord Henry his brother after him, as he bears witness who was there and saw it and heard it, Robert of Clari, knight. And he has made the truth to be put in writing, how it was conquered. And though it may be that he has not told the conquest as finely as many a good teller would have told it, none the less he has told the very truth, and there are so many true things that he cannot remember them all.

Appendix

Appendix

Note on the Fleet and the Forces

WHEN the envoys made the treaty with Venice, they contracted for a fleet to carry 4,500 knights and their horses, 9,000 squires, and 20,000 foot soldiers, but when the crusaders were gathered at Venice, according to Villehardouin, the fleet proved to be three times as large as was needed, because so many had gone to other ports. Taken literally, this would mean that about 11,000 armed men turned up at Venice to go oversea. This number was reduced by later defections and losses in fighting at Constantinople, so that the armed forces of the crusaders at the time of the capture of the city could not have been more than 10,000. Thus Villehardouin later expatiates on the marvel that some 20,000 fighting men, crusaders and Venetians together, conquered a city defended by 400,000 Greeks.

If there were around 10,000 crusaders of combatant ranks, and the proportions of the ranks were those indicated in the treaty, then there would have been about 1,300 knights, 2,600 sergeants on horse, and 6,000 foot soldiers. This agrees rather neatly with the evidence of Villehardouin and of the *Devastatio* regarding the division of the 100,000 marks of spoil. In this division, Villehardouin says, two sergeants on foot were considered equal to one mounted sergeant and two mounted sergeants equivalent to one knight. For 10,000 men, this would work out to about 24 marks to a knight, 12 marks to a mounted sergeant, and 6 marks to a sergeant on foot. Now the *Devastatio* says that they gave 20 marks to each knight, 10 marks to each mounted sergeant and each cleric, and 5 marks to each sergeant on foot.

In his letter to the duke of Louvain, Hugh of St. Pol gives an estimate of the crusading forces engaged in the battle of

July, 1203, in which he himself commanded one of the divisions, along with his cousin Pierre of Amiens. He says that in the attacking divisions there were only 500 knights, as many squires, and 2,000 foot soldiers, "for the greater part had been set to guard our engines." This would make about 3,000 men in the three attacking divisions and 4,000 or 5,000 in the other four, but if we take as a basis the number of knights, 500 in the attacking divisions and 700 or 800 in the others, we arrive at a figure close to 10,000 men, the difference being due to Hugh's error in respect to the relative number of knights and mounted sergeants in the "battles." Thus the estimate of 10,000 armed crusaders is probably not far from the facts.[1]

Contemporary accounts of the expedition generally agree in describing the fleet as made up of three types of vessels: galleys (*galees, galiae*), "ships" (*nes, naves*), and horse transports (*uissiers, usariae*).[2] The galleys were the fighting convoys, long narrow vessels propelled by oars, with auxiliary sails. The galley of this time was about 100 feet over all, and it carried a crew, mariners and rowers, of more than 100, and a certain number of marines, largely archers and crossbowmen. The ships were the large merchant vessels or freighters, converted into transports. They were sailing vessels, usually two-masters and two-deckers, broad in the beam, and capable, some of them, of carrying a thousand passengers or more. Although ships of this size are mentioned in the sources, they were probably exceptional, and we need not suppose that all the transports furnished by the Venetians were as large as this. Probably there were only a few of these great ships, built especially for the leaders, and bearing each its own name, like the *Paradisus* of the bishop of Soissons, the *Peregrina* of the bishop of Troyes, the *Viola* of Stephen of Perche, mentioned in the *Devastatio*, and the *Aquila* of the Venetians, mentioned by Dandulo. Rob-

---

[1] Robert's figures of a hundred knights in each of the seven battles is not to be taken literally, since he generally uses his figures impressionistically.

[2] See Byrne, *Genoese Shipping*, chaps. 1, 2, 3; De la Roncière, *Histoire de la marine française*, I, 243 ff.; Jal, *Archéologie navale*, and *Glossaire nautique*. Enlart, *Manuel d'archéologie*, II, chap. 5, derives mainly from De la Roncière.

ert says that there were only four or five ships in the fleet that were high enough to reach the wooden towers which the Greeks had built on the walls. The horse transports, or *uissiers* (so-named from the *huis* or door in the side), belonged, it seems, to the general type of the galley; they were long narrow vessels propelled by oars, with space in the shallow hold for a number of horses. Jal [3] reckons that the *uissier* of this time carried about 40 horses and 80 squires, in addition to the crew.

There are three contemporary accounts by eyewitnesses that mention the number of vessels in the fleet. The most definite is the one given in the *Devastatio,* which is generally accurate and circumstantial. Describing the fleet as it left the harbor of Venice in October, 1202, this account says that there were 40 ships (*naves*), 62 galleys (*galiae*), and 100 horse transports (*oxorii*). It mentions specifically the loss of four ships and two transports. The total agrees remarkably with that of the fleet on its arrival before Constantinople, June, 1203, as given in the letter of Hugh of St. Pol: ships, galleys, and transports to the number of 200, not counting the barges and skiffs. Nicetas says that the fleet prepared by the Venetians for the expedition comprised 110 horse transports, 60 long ships (galleys), and more than 70 round ships, of which one was so large that it was called the *World* (*Kosmos*).[4]

[3] *Archéologie navale,* I, 480.
[4] The fourteenth-century Venetian chronicler Dandulo, who may have drawn his information from sources nearly contemporary with the event, gives the number of vessels that sailed out from the harbor of Venice as nearly 300 (*tercentorum enim navigiorum fere stolus erat*).

Bibliography

Bibliography

Sources

Alberic of Trois-Fontaines. Chronica. Editions: P. Scheffer-Boichorst, Monumenta Germaniae Historica: Scriptores, XXIII, 674-950. M.-J.-J. Brial, Recueil des historiens des Gaules et de la France, XVIII, 745-96. (Extract.)

Anonymous of Halberstadt. Peregrinatio in Graeciam. Ed. by Riant in Exuviae sacrae Constantinopolitanae, I, 10-21. Geneva, 1877.

Anonymous of Soissons. De terra Iherosolimitana. Ed. by Riant in Exuviae sacrae Constantinopolitanae, I, 1-9. Geneva, 1877.

Anthony of Novgorod. Le Livre du pélerin, trad. par Mme. B. de Khitrowo pour la Société d'Orient latin, in Itinéraires russes, I, i, 87-111. 1889. There is another translation into French by Marcelle Ehrard, pub. in Romania, LVIII (1932), 44-65; and a Latin translation in Riant, Exuviae, II, 218-30.

Benedict of Peterborough. Gesta regis Henrici secundi Benedicti abbatis. Ed. by W. Stubbs. London, 1867. "Rolls Series," XLIX.

Chronista Novgorodensis. Latin translation in Hopf, Chroniques gréco-romanes, pp. 93-98. Berlin, 1873.

Comnena, Anna. Alexias. Ed. by A. Reifferscheid. Leipzig, Teubner, 1884. There is an English translation: The Alexiad of the Princess Anna Comnena . . . trans. by E. A. S. Dawes, London, Kegan Paul, 1928.

Dandulo. Andreae Danduli Venetorum ducis chronicon Venetum a pontificatu sancti Marci ad annum 1339. In Rerum Italicarum scriptores, XII, cols. 13-416. Milan, 1728.

Devastatio Constantinopolitana. Editions: Pertz, M. G. H. SS., XVI, 9-12. Hopf, Chroniques gréco-romanes, pp. 86-92.

Eracles. L'Estoire de Eracles empereur. In Recueil des historiens des croisades. Historiens occidentaux, I, II. Paris, Imprimérie impériale, 1844-1859.

Ernoul. Chronique d'Ernoul et de Bernard le Trésorier. Ed. by L. de Mas Latrie. Paris, Renouard, 1871. "Société de l'histoire de France."

Gesta Innocentii tertii, ab auctore anonymo, sed coaetano scripta. Ed. in Migne, Patrologia Latina, CCXIV, cols. xvii-ccxxviii. Paris, 1890.

Guillaume le Breton. See Rigord.

Gunther of Pairis. Historia Constantinopolitana. Ed. by Riant in Exuviae sacrae Constantinopolitanae, I, 57-126. Geneva, 1877.

Nicetas Acominatos Choniates. Historia. Editions: Imm. Bekker, Corpus Scriptorum historiae Byzantinae. Bonn, Weber, 1835. Migne, Patrologia Graeca, CXXXIX. Paris, 1894.

Pierre of Vaux-de-Cernay. Petri Vallium Sarnaii monachi hystoria Albigensis. Ed. by Pascal Guebin and Ernest Lyon. 2 vols. Paris, Champion, 1926, 1930. "Société de l'histoire de France."

Rigord. Œuvres de Rigord et de Guillaume le Breton. Ed. by H. F. Delaborde. Vol. I. Paris, Renouard, 1882. "Société de l'histoire de France."

Ralph of Coggeshall. Radulphi de Coggeshall, Chronicon Anglicanum. Ed. by J. Stevenson. London, 1875. "Rolls Series," LXVI.

Récits d'un ménestrel de Reims au treizième siècle. Ed. by N. de Wailly. Paris, Renouard, 1876. "Société de l'histoire de France."

Robert of Auxerre. Chronologia. "Recueil des historiens des Gaules et de la France," XVIII, 247-90. (Extract.)

Robert of Clari. Editions and translations:

 Paul Riant. Li Estoires de chiaus qui conquisent Constantinople, de Robert de Clari en Aminois, chevalier. Paris, 1868 (?). (Incomplete, unpublished, a few copies distributed privately.)

 Charles Hopf. Chroniques gréco-romanes. Berlin, Weidmann, 1873, pp. 1-85.

 Philippe Lauer. Robert de Clari. La Conquête de Constantinople. Paris, Champion, 1924. "Les Classiques français du moyen âge."

 B. Todt. Die Eroberung von Constantinopel im Jahre 1204. Halle, 1878. (German translation of passages from Villehardouin and Robert of Clari.)

 B. Zeller. L'Empire français d'orient: la IVᵉ Croisade, 1199-1205. Extraits de Villehardouin, de Robert de Clari, etc. Paris, Hachette, 1885. "L'Histoire de France racontée par les contemporains." (French translation of selected passages.)

Synaxarium ecclesiae Constantinopolitanae e codice Sirmondiano, ed. Delehaye. Propylaeum ad Acta sanctorum Novembris. Bruxellis, apud socios Bollandianos, 1902.

Tafel, G. L. Fr., and G. M. Thomas. Urkunden zur älteren Handels- und Staatsgeschichte der Republik Venedig, mit besonderer Beziehung auf Byzanz und die Levante. 2 vols. Vienna, K.-k. Hof- und Staatsdruckerei, 1856. "Fontes rerum Austriacarum." 2. Abtheilung, XII. Band.

Bibliography 139

Villehardouin, Editions and translations:

Charles du Fresne du Cange. Histoire de l'empire de Constantinople sous les empereurs françois, divisée en deux parties dont la première contient l'histoire de la conquête de la ville de Constantinople par les François et les Vénitiens, écrite par Geoffroy de Villehardouin. Paris, Imprimérie royale, 1657.

J. A. Bouchon. Chronique de la prise de Constantinople par les Francs, écrite par Geoffroy de Villehardouin, maréchal de France et de Romanie. Paris, Firmin-Didot, 1828. "Collection des chroniques nationales françaises," 3.

Paulin Paris. De la conqueste de Constantinople, par Joffroi de Villehardouin et Henri de Valenciennes. Paris, Renouard, 1838. "Société de l'histoire de France."

N. De Wailly. La Conquête de Constantinople, par Geoffroy de Villehardouin. Texte original accompagné d'une traduction. Paris, Firmin-Didot, 1872.

Emile Bouchet. Geoffroi de Villehardouin, La Conquête de Constantinople. Texte et traduction nouvelle. 2 vols. Paris, Lemerre, 1891.

The Chronicle of Geoffrey de Villehardouin, marshal of Champagne. Trans. by T. Smith. London, Pickering, 1829.

Memoirs of the Crusades by Villehardouin and de Joinville. Trans. by F. Marzials. London and Toronto, Dent; New York, Dutton, 1908. "Everyman's Library," pp. 1-133.

Authorities

Abrahams, N. C. L. Description des manuscrits français du moyen âge de la Bibliothèque royale de Copenhague. Copenhagen, Thiele, 1844.

Banduri, Anselmus. Imperium orientale sive antiquitates Constantinopolitanae in quatuor partes distributae. Tomus primus. Paris, Coignard, 1711.

Boudon, G. "Robert de Clari en Aminois." Bulletin de la Société des antiquaires de Picardie, XIX (1895-97), 700-734.

—— "Documents nouveaux sur la famille de Robert de Clari." Ibid., XX (1899), 372-79.

Bruun, Christian. Det store kongelige Bibliotheks Stiftelse under Kong Frederik den Tredie og Kong Christian den Femte. I Anledning af Bibliothekets tohunderaarige Jubilaeum. Copenhagen, Thiele, 1873.

Byrne, Eugene. Genoese Shipping in the Twelfth and Thirteenth Centuries. Cambridge, Mass., 1930. "Monographs of the Mediaeval Academy of America."

Chalandon, Ferdinand. Jean II Comnène et Manuel I Comnène. Paris, Picard, 1912.

Chambon, Félix. "Un Historien peu connu de la quatrième croisade— Robert de Clari." Bulletin de l'Académie des sciences, belles lettres, et arts de Clermont-Ferrand, 2ᵉ série, 1897, Mélanges, pp. 264-77.

Coquelin, Dom Benedict. Historiae regalis abbatiae Corbeiensis compendium. Auctore Dom. Benedicto Coquelin, eiusdem abbatiae officiali seu fori ecclesiastici contentiosi prefecto, ab ann. 1672 ad ann. 1678. Edidit et annotavit J. Garnier. Amiens, Duval et Herment, 1846. "Mémoires de la Société des antiquaires de Picardie." VIII.

Diehl, Charles. Figures byzantines. 2 vols. Paris, Colin, 1925.

——— Manuel d'art byzantin. 2 vols. 2d ed. Paris, Picard, 1925, 1926.

——— Justinien et la civilization byzantine au sixième siècle. Paris, Leroux, 1901.

Du Cange, Charles du Fresne. Historia Byzantina duplici commentario illustrata. Prior familias ac stemmata imperatorum Constantinopolitanorum . . . complectitur; alter descriptionem urbis Constantinopolitanae, qualiter extitit sub imperatoribus Christianis. Paris, Billaine, 1680.

——— Histoire de l'état et de la ville d'Amiens et de ses comtes . . . ouvrage inédit. Ed. by H. Hardouin. Amiens, Duval et Herment, 1840.

——— Traité historique du chef de S. Jean-Baptiste. Paris, Cramoisy, 1665.

Dusevel, H., ed. Histoire abrégée du trésor de l'abbaye royale de St. Pierre de Corbie (ca. 1673). Nouvelle édition. Amiens, Lemer, 1861.

Ebersolt, Jean. Le Grand Palais et le Livre des Cérémonies. Paris, Leroux, 1910. Bibliothèque de la fondation Thiers, XXI.

——— Constantinople byzantine et les voyageurs du Levant. Paris, Leroux, 1918.

——— Sanctuaires de Byzance. Paris, Leroux, 1921.

——— Monuments d'architecture byzantine. Paris, Van Oest, 1934.

Enlart, C. Manuel d'archéologie française depuis les temps mérovingiens jusqu'à la renaissance. Vol. II. Paris, Picard, 1904.

Erichsen, John. Udsigt over den gamle Manuscript-Samling i det store Kongelige Bibliothek. Copenhagen, Møller, 1786.

Gerland, Ernst. "Der vierte Kreuzzug und seine Probleme." Neue Jahrbücher für das klassische Altertum und für Pädagogik, XIII (1904), Klass. Altertum, 505-14.

———— Geschichte des lateinischen Kaiserreiches von Konstantinopel. I. Teil: Geschichte der Kaiser Balduin I. und Heinrich, 1204-1216. Homburg, 1905. "Geschichte der Frankenherrschaft in Griechenland, II."

Gilles, Pierre. Petri Gylii de topographia Constantinopoleos et de illius antiquitatibus libri quatuor. Lyons, Roville, 1561.

Grenier, Dom. Histoire de la ville et du comté de Corbie. Publié par MM. H. Josse, A. de Calonne, et Cl. Brunel. Amiens, Yvert et Tellier; Paris, Picard, 1910. "Société des antiquaires de Picardie. Fondation Henri Debray. Documents inédits sur l'abbaye, Je comté, et la ville de Corbie," I.

Gutsch, Milton. "A Twelfth Century Preacher—Fulk of Neuilly." The Crusades and other Historical Essays, presented to Dana C. Munro. Ed. by Louis J. Paetow. New York, Crofts, 1928.

Hanotaux, G. "Les Vénitiens ont-ils trahi la chrétienté en 1202?" Revue historique, IV (1877), 74-102.

Heisenberg, August. Grabeskirche und Apostelkirche: Zwei Basiliken Konstantins. Erster Teil: Die Grabeskirche in Jerusalem. Zweiter Teil: Die Apostelkirche in Konstantinopel. Leipzig, Hinrichs, 1908.

———— ed. Nikolaos Mesarites. Die Palastrevolution des Johannes Komnenos. "Prog. des k. alten Gymn. zu Würzburg." 1907.

Heyd, Wilhelm. Geschichte des Levantehandels im Mittelalter. 2 vols. Stuttgart, Cotta, 1879. (French translation of revised edition, by Furcy Raynaud, Histoire du commerce du Levant au moyen âge. Réimpression. Leipzig, Harrassowitz, 1923.)

Hopf, Karl. Geschichte Griechenlands: Griechenland im Mittelalter und in der Neuzeit. Leipzig, Brockhaus, 1867. Allgemeine Encyclopädie der Wissenschaft und Kunste . . . herausgegeben von J. S. Ersch und J. G. Gruber, Vols. 85, 86.

Ilgen, Theodor. Markgraf Conrad von Montferrat. Marburg, Elwert, 1880.

Iorga, N. Histoire de la vie byzantine. Empire et civilization. 3 vols. Vol. 3, L'Empire et la pénétration latine (1081-1453). Bucarest, 1934.

Jal, Auguste. Archéologie navale. 2 vols. Paris, Bertrand, 1840.

———— Glossaire nautique; répertoire polyglotte de termes de marine anciens et modernes. Paris, Firmin-Didot, 1848.

Jeanroy, A. "La Conquête de Constantinople de Robert de Clari, ed. Ph. Lauer." Romania, LIII (1927), 392-93.

Kandel, M. "Quelques observations sur la 'Devastatio Constantino-politana.'" Byzantion, IV (1927-28), 179-88.

Klimke, C. Die Quellen zur Geschichte des vierten Kreuzzuges. Breslau, Aderholz, 1875. Dissertation.

Krause, J. H. Die Eroberungen von Konstantinopel im dreizehnten und fünfzehnten Jahrhundert. Halle, Schwetzschke's Verlag, 1870.

Lethaby, W. R., and Swainson, H. The Church of Sancta Sophia, Constantinople; a study of Byzantine building. Macmillan, London and New York, 1894.

Luchaire, A. Innocent III: la question d'Orient. Paris, Hachette, 1907.

McNeal, E. H. "The Story of Isaac and Andronicus." Speculum, IX (1934), 324-29.

Mas Latrie, L. de. Histoire de l'Ile de Chypre sous le règne des princes de la maison de Lusignan. 3 vols. Paris, Imprimérie impériale, 1852-1861.

Mély, F. de. Exuviae sacrae Constantinopolitanae. La croix des premiers croisés; la sainte lance; la sainte couronne. Paris, Leroux, 1904.

Meyer, Paul. Annuaire-Bulletin de la Société de l'histoire de France. Année 1890. Discours de M. Paul Meyer, Président de la Société. (Pp. 82-106.)

———— Revue critique d'histoire et de littérature, 6ᵉ année, 2ᵉ sem., 1872, 395-96.

Moeser, H. Gottfried von Ville-Hardouin und der Lateinerzug gen Byzanz. Breslau, Nischkowsky, 1897. Inaugural-Dissertation, Bern.

Muralt, E. de. Essai de chronographie byzantine, 1057-1453. 2 vols. Basle and Geneva, H. Georg; St. Petersburg, Eggers, 1871-1873.

Neumann, C. "Die byzantinische Marine." Historische Zeitschrift, N. F. XLV (1898), 1-23.

Norden, W. Der vierte Kreuzzug im Rahmen der Beziehungen des Abendlandes zu Byzanz. II. Abschnitt: Die Wendung des vierten Kreuzzugs gegen Constantinopel war nicht das Werk einer Intrigue. Berlin, Stankiewicz, 1898. Inaugural-Dissertation, Berlin.

———— Das Papsttum und Byzanz. Berlin, Behr, 1903.

Nyrop, K. "Un Nouveau Manuscrit de la chronique de Reims." Romania, VIII (1879), 429-33.

———— "Zu Robert von Clari." Zeitschrift für romanische Philologie, III (1879), 96-98.

Paris, Gaston. De pseudo-Turpino disseruit Gaston Paris, juris litterarumque licentiatus in schola chartarum quondam alumnus. Paris, A. Franck, 1865.

Pauphilet, A. "Robert de Clari et Villehardouin." Mélanges de linguistique et de littérature offerts à M. Jeanroy par ses élèves et ses amis. Abbéville, Imprimérie F. Pouillet; Paris, Droz, 1928.

——— "Sur Robert de Clari." Romania, LVII (1931), 289-311.

Pears, E. The Fall of Constantinople, Being the Story of the Fourth Crusade. New York, Harpers, 1886.

Quignon, G. H. Un Historien picard de la quatrième croisade; Robert de Clari. Cayeux-sur-Mer, Ollivier, 1908. "Collection des Rosati picards d'Amiens." XXIX.

Rambaud, A. "Robert de Clari, guerrier et historien de la quatrième croisade." Mémoires de l'Académie nationale des sciences, arts, et belles lettres de Caen, 1873, 110-44.

Riant, Comte Paul. Des Dépouilles religieuses enlevées à Constantinople au XIIIᵉ siècle par les Latins, et des documents historiques nés de leur transport en occident. Paris, 1875. "Extraits des Mémoires de la Société nationale des antiquaires de France," XXXVI.

——— "Innocent III, Philippe de Souabe, et Boniface de Montferrat." Revue des questions historiques, XVII (1875), 321-74; XVIII (1875), 1-75.

——— "Le Changement de direction de la quatrième croisade." Revue des questions historiques, XXIII (1878), 71-114.

Richter, J. P. Quellen der byzantinischen Kunstgeschichte. Vienna, Graeser, 1897.

Roncière, Charles de la. Histoire de la marine française. 2 vols. Paris, Plon-Nourrit, 1899.

Runciman, Steven. "Some Remarks on the Image of Edessa." Cambridge Historical Journal, 1931, pp. 232-52.

Streit, L. Commentatio de auctoribus IV belli sacri. Putbusii, 1863.

——— Venedig und die Wendung des vierten Kreuzzuges gegen Konstantinopel. Anklam, Krüger, 1877. "Beiträge zur Geschichte des vierten Kreuzzuges," I.

Strzygowski, J. "Das goldne Thor in Konstantinopel." Jahrbuch des kaiserlich-deutschen archäologischen Instituts, VIII, 1-39.

——— "Die Säule des Arkadius in Konstantinopel." Ibid., pp. 230-49.

Tessier, J. La Quatrième Croisade. Paris, Leroux, 1884.

Tixeront, L.-J. Les Origines de l'église d'Édesse et la légende d'Abgar. Paris, Maisonneuve et Leclerc, 1888.

Unger, Fr. W. Quellen der byzantinischen Kunstgeschichte. Ausgezogen und übersetzt von Friedrich Wilhelm Unger. Vienna, Braumüller, 1878. "Quellenschriften für Kunstgeschichte und Kunsttechnik des Mittelalters und der Renaissance," XII.

Van Millingen, A. Byzantine Constantinople. London, Macmillan, 1899.

——— Byzantine Churches in Constantinople; Their History and Architecture. London, Macmillan, 1912.

Vasiliev, A. A. History of the Byzantine Empire. 2 vols. Madison, 1927, 1929. "University of Wisconsin Studies in the Social Sciences and History."

Vriens, H. "De Kwestie van den vierden Kruistocht." Tijdschrift voor Geschiednis, XXXV (1922), 50-82.

Waitz, Georg. "Untersuchung der handschriftlichen Sammlungen zu Copenhagen im Herbste, 1836." Archiv der Gesellschaft für ältere deutsche Geschichtskunde, VII (1839), 146-67.

Wallensköld, A. Les Chansons de Conon de Béthune. Paris, Champion, 1921. "Les Classiques français du moyen âge."

Wanner, E. Robert de Clari, ein altfranzösischer Chronist des IV. Kreuzzuges. Schaffhausen, Schoch, 1901. Inaugural-Dissertation, Zürich.

Winkelmann, E. Philipp von Schwaben und Otto IV. von Braunschweig. I. König Philipp von Schwaben. Leipzig, Duncker und Humblot, 1873. "Jahrbücher der deutschen Geschichte."

Index

Index

Clarembaux of Chappes, 32
Comans, 87-88, 122, 125, 127
Conon of Béthune, 13, 32, 36, 83, 121
Conrad, bishop of Halberstadt, 3, 32, 94, 114
Conrad, marquis of Montferrat, 15, 18, 19-21, 25, 35, 59-65
Constantine the Great, 16, 102, 108
Constantinople, description of, 16-18, 67, 101-13; first attack on, 67-77; taking of, 92-101
Corbie, 38; monastery of, 5, 6, 7, 9; castellán of, 33
Corfu, 14, 58, 125
Coucy, castellan of, 32
Crete, 125
Crown of Thorns, 103
curre, 109

Dandulo, Andrew, chronicle of, references to, 43, 44, 69, 92, 114, 132, 133
Dandulo, Henry, *see* Doge of Venice
Danes (in Constantinople), 95, 100
De excidio Troiae, 8
Demetrius, saint, 127; miraculous portrait of, 17, 105
Devastatio Constantinopolitana, 3; references to, 31, 41, 43, 90, 117, 131-33
Doge of Venice (Henry Dandulo), 14, 22, 37-45, 58-59, 66, 67, 68, 70, 71, 78, 83-84, 113-14, 118, 120, 121, 124, 125-126
dromons, 39

Edessa, *see* Image of Edessa
English (in Constantinople), 95, 100
Enguerrand of Boves, 32, 44
Ernoul, chronicle of, 3, 20, 24
Eustace of Canteleux, 32, 74
Eustace of Heumont, 33

Flagellation, column of, 16, 108
Forum of the Augusteion, 107
Forum of Theodosius, 111
Forum of the Xerolophos, 111
Frederick Barbarossa, 111
Fulk of Neuilly, 25, 31, 34, 38

Galata, tower of, 69, 70, 80, 97
Gate of St. Romanus, 71
Gate of the Golden Mantle, 17, 108
Genoa, 36, 37
Genoese (in Tyre), 63-65

Geoffrey of Villehardouin, 32, 36, 83, 121; chronicle of, 3, 16, 24; references to, 12, 13, 15, 31, 36, 38, 43, 44, 45, 46, 58, 69, 72, 74, 82, 83, 92, 95, 96, 100, 101, 111, 114, 121, 124, 131
Gervais of the Châtel, 33
Gesta Innocentii tertii, 3
Gilbert of Vismes, 34
Giles of Aulnoy, 33
Gilo, father of Robert of Clari, 4-5
Girard of Manchecourt, 32
Golden Gate, 16, 17, 108-9, 111
Golden Horn, 54, 69, 73, 82, 94, 100
Great Palace, *see* Boukoleon, palace of
Gunther of Pairis, *Historia Constantinopolitana*, 3, 21; references to, 31, 100, 111, 124
Guy of Lusignan, king of Jerusalem, 62-65
Guy of Manchecourt, 34
Guy of Montfort, 31

Helena, mother of Constantine, 16, 108
Henry, count of Champagne, king of Jerusalem, 65
Henry of Flanders (Emperor Henry), 6, 7, 31, 33, 72-75, 88-91, 122, 125, 126-28; election, 126; death, 128
Heraclius, emperor, 17, 107
Hervé of the Châtel, 33
Hippodrome, 16, 18, 82, 102, 109-10
Hodogetria, church of the, 90
Holy Apostles, church of the, 16, 108
Holy Chapel, *see* Blessed Virgin of the Pharos, church of the
Holy Land, 3, 13, 19, 20, 25, 31, 34, 44, 60
Hospitallers, 62
Hugh, count of St. Pol, 4, 15, 31, 72-75, 113, 114, 116, 117-18, 124, 125; letter of, 13, 15, 22, 66, 69, 70, 131, 133
Hugh of Boves, 32
Hugh of Bracheux, 33
Humphrey of Thoron, 62, 65

icon, 26, 89-91
Image of Edessa, 17, 104
Image of Our Lady, 126
Innocent III, pope, 31, 43, 45, 88; letters of, 86, 88, 127
Irene, wife of Philip of Swabia, 46, 57
Isaac II Angelus, emperor, 18, 19, 20, 26, 46, 51-57, 60, 77-85, 111